Microsoft

T0351206

MOS Study Guide for Microsoft Excel Exam MO-200

Joan Lambert

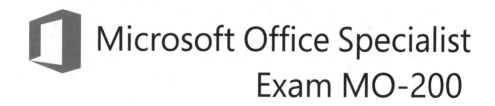
Microsoft Office Specialist
Exam MO-200

MOS Study Guide for Microsoft Excel Exam MO-200

Published with the authorization of Microsoft Corporation by:
Pearson Education, Inc.

ISBN-13: 978-0-13-662715-9
ISBN-10: 0-13-662715-3

Library of Congress Control Number: 2020931638

1 2020

Trademarks

Warning and Disclaimer

Special Sales

For information about buying this title in bulk quantities, or for special sales opportunities (which may include electronic versions; custom cover designs; and content particular to your business, training goals, marketing focus, or branding interests), please contact our corporate sales department at corpsales@pearsoned.com or (800) 382-3419.

For government sales inquiries, please contact governmentsales@pearsoned.com.

For questions about sales outside the U.S., please contact intlcs@pearson.com.

Editor-in-Chief
Brett Bartow

Executive Editor
Loretta Yates

Development Editor
Songlin Qiu

Sponsoring Editor
Charvi Arora

Managing Editor
Sandra Schroeder

Senior Project Editor
Tracey Croom

Copy Editor
Dan Foster

Indexer
Cheryl Ann Lenser

Proofreader
Abigail Manheim

Technical Editor
Boyd Nolan

Editorial Assistant
Cindy Teeters

Cover Designer
Twist Creative, Seattle

Compositor
codeMantra

Contents

Introduction

The Microsoft Office Specialist (MOS) certification program has been designed to validate your knowledge of and ability to use programs in the Microsoft Office suite of programs. This book has been designed to guide you in studying the types of tasks you are likely to be required to demonstrate in Exam MO-200: Microsoft Excel 2019.

See Also For information about the tasks you are likely to be required to demonstrate in Exam MO-201: Microsoft Excel 2019 Expert, see *MOS 2019 Study Guide for Microsoft Excel Expert* by Paul McFedries (Microsoft Press, 2020).

Who this book is for

MOS 2019 Study Guide for Microsoft Excel is designed for experienced computer users seeking Microsoft Office Specialist certification in Excel 2019 or the equivalent version of Excel for Office 365.

MOS exams for individual programs are practical rather than theoretical. You must demonstrate that you can complete certain tasks or projects rather than simply answer questions about program features. The successful MOS certification candidate will have at least six months of experience using all aspects of the application on a regular basis—for example, using Excel at work or school to create and manage workbooks and worksheets, modify and format cell content, summarize and organize data, present data in tables and charts, perform data operations by using functions and formulas, and insert and format objects on worksheets.

As a certification candidate, you probably have a lot of experience with the program for which you want to become certified. Many of the procedures described in this book will be familiar to you; others might not be. Read through each study section and ensure that you are familiar with the procedures, concepts, and tools discussed. In some cases, images depict the tools you will use to perform procedures related to the skill set. Study the images and ensure that you are familiar with the options available for each tool.

How this book is organized

The exam coverage is divided into chapters representing broad skill sets that correlate to the functional groups covered by the exam. Each chapter is divided into sections addressing groups of related skills that correlate to the exam objectives. Each section includes review information, generic procedures, and practice tasks you can complete on your own while studying. We provide practice files you can use to work through the practice tasks, and results files you can use to check your work. You can practice the generic procedures in this book by using the practice files supplied or by using your own files.

Throughout this book, you will find Exam Strategy tips that present information about the scope of study that is necessary to ensure that you achieve mastery of a skill set and are successful in your certification effort.

Download the practice files

Before you can complete the practice tasks in this book, you need to copy the book's practice files and results files to your computer. Download the compressed (zipped) folder from the following page, and extract the files from it to a folder (such as your Documents folder) on your computer:

MicrosoftPressStore.com/MOSExcel200/downloads

IMPORTANT The Excel 2019 program is not available from this website. You should purchase and install that program before using this book.

You will save the completed versions of practice files that you modify while working through the practice tasks in this book. If you later want to repeat the practice tasks, you can download the original practice files again.

The following table lists the practice files provided for this book.

Folder and objective group	Practice files	Result files
MOSExcel2019\Objective1 Manage worksheets and workbooks	Excel_1-1.xlsx	Excel_1-1_Results subfolder: • Excel_1-1_results.xlsx • MyBlank_results.xlsx • MyCalc_results.xlsx
	Excel_1-2.xlsx	Excel_1-2_results.xlsx
	Excel_1-3.xlsx	Excel_1-3_results.xlsx
	Excel_1-4.xlsx	Excel_1-4_results.xlsx
	Excel_1-5.xlsx	Excel_1-5_Results subfolder: • Excel_1-5a_results.xlsx • MOS-Compatible.xls • MOS-Template.xltm
MOSExcel2019\Objective2 Manage data cells and ranges	Excel_2-1.xlsx	Excel_2-1_results.xlsx
	Excel_2-2.xlsx	Excel_2-2_results.xlsx
	Excel_2-3.xlsx	Excel_2-3_results.xlsx
MOSExcel2019\Objective3 Manage tables and table data	Excel_3-1.xlsx	Excel_3-1_results.xlsx
	Excel_3-2.xlsx	Excel_3-2_results.xlsx
	Excel_3-3.xlsx	Excel_3-3_results.xlsx
MOSExcel2019\Objective4 Perform operations by using formulas and functions	Excel_4-1a.xlsx	Excel_4-1a_results.xlsx
	Excel_4-1b.xlsx	Excel_4-1b_results.xlsx
	Excel_4-1c.xlsx	Excel_4-1c_results.xlsx
	Excel_4-2.xlsx	Excel_4-2_results.xlsx
	Excel_4-3.xlsx	Excel_4-3_results.xlsx
MOSExcel2019\Objective5 Manage charts	Excel_5-1.xlsx	Excel_5-1_results.xlsx
	Excel_5-2.xlsx	Excel_5-2_results.xlsx
	Excel_5-3a.xlsx	Excel_5-3_results.xlsx
	Excel_5-3b.jpg	
	Excel_5-3c.txt	

Adapt procedure steps

This book contains many images of user interface elements that you'll work with while performing tasks in Excel on a Windows computer. Depending on your screen resolution or app window width, the Excel ribbon on your screen might look different from that shown in this book. (If you turn on Touch mode, the ribbon displays significantly fewer commands than in Mouse mode.) As a result, procedural instructions that involve the ribbon might require a little adaptation.

Simple procedural instructions use this format:

- On the **Insert** tab, in the **Illustrations** group, click the **Chart** button.

If the command is in a list, our instructions use this format:

- On the **Home** tab, in the **Editing** group, click the **Find** arrow and then, in the **Find** list, click **Go To**.

If differences between your display settings and ours cause a button to appear differently on your screen than it does in this book, you can easily adapt the steps to locate the command. First click the specified tab, and then locate the specified group. If a group has been collapsed into a group list or under a group button, click the list or button to display the group's commands. If you can't immediately identify the button you want, point to likely candidates to display their names in ScreenTips.

The instructions in this book assume that you're interacting with on-screen elements on your computer by clicking (with a mouse, touchpad, or other hardware device). If you're using a different method—for example, if your computer has a touchscreen interface and you're tapping the screen (with your finger or a stylus)—substitute the applicable tapping action when you interact with a user interface element.

Instructions in this book refer to user interface elements that you click or tap on the screen as *buttons*, and to physical buttons that you press on a keyboard as *keys*, to conform to the standard terminology used in documentation for these products.

Ebook edition

If you're reading the ebook edition of this book, you can do the following:

- Search the full text
- Print
- Copy and paste

You can purchase and download the ebook edition from the Microsoft Press Store at:

MicrosoftPressStore.com/MOSExcel200/detail

Errata, updates, & book support

We've made every effort to ensure the accuracy of this book and its companion content. If you discover an error, please submit it to us through the link at:

MicrosoftPressStore.com/MOSExcel200/errata

For additional book support and information, please visit:

www.MicrosoftPressStore.com/Support

Please note that product support for Microsoft software and hardware is not offered through the previous addresses. For help with Microsoft software or hardware, go to:

https://support.microsoft.com

Stay in touch

Let's keep the conversation going! We're on Twitter at:

https://twitter.com/MicrosoftPress

About the author

JOAN LAMBERT has worked closely with Microsoft technologies since 1986, and in the training and certification industry since 1997, guiding the translation of technical information and requirements into useful, relevant, and measurable resources for people who are seeking certification of their computer skills or who simply want to get things done efficiently.

Joan is the author or coauthor of more than four dozen books about Windows and Office (for Windows, Mac, and iPad), six generations of Microsoft Office Specialist certification study guides, video-based training courses for SharePoint and OneNote, QuickStudy guides for Windows 10 and Office 2016, and GO! series books for Outlook.

Joan is a Microsoft Certified Professional, Microsoft Office Specialist Master (for all versions of Office since Office 2003), Microsoft Certified Technology Specialist (for Windows and Windows Server), Microsoft Certified Technology Associate (for Windows), Microsoft Dynamics Specialist, and Microsoft Certified Trainer. She is also certified in Adobe InDesign and Intuit QuickBooks.

A native of the Pacific Northwest and enthusiastic world traveler, Joan is now blissfully based in America's Finest City with her simply divine daughter Trinity, Thai host daughter Thopad, and their faithful canine, feline, and aquatic companions.

Objective group 1

Manage worksheets and workbooks

The skills tested in this section of the Microsoft Office Specialist exam for Microsoft Excel 2019 relate to the basic management of workbooks and worksheets. Specifically, the following objectives are associated with this set of skills:

- **1.1** Import data into workbooks
- **1.2** Navigate within workbooks
- **1.3** Format worksheets and workbooks
- **1.4** Customize options and views
- **1.5** Configure content for collaboration

A single workbook can contain a vast amount of raw and calculated data stored on one or more worksheets. The data on a worksheet can be independent or related to data in other areas of the workbook or in other workbooks.

You can structure and format workbook content so that key information can be easily identified and so that data is presented correctly on the screen and when printed. You can locate information within a workbook by searching text, values, formula elements, or named objects.

This chapter guides you in studying ways of importing data into workbooks; finding specific text, formatting, or named worksheet content; linking to content within and outside of a workbook; setting up worksheet pages, headers, and footers; modifying the Quick Access Toolbar; changing the display of workbook and worksheet content; and preparing workbook content to share with other people.

Objective 1.1: Import data into workbooks

Import data from delimited text files

There are several ways to enter information into a workbook:

- You can populate worksheets by entering text directly into them.

- If the content you want to use exists in a tabular format, such as a Microsoft Word table, you can copy it from the source and paste it into a worksheet.

- If the content you want to use exists in a delimited data format, you can import the file contents into Excel.

Entering text directly into a worksheet and pasting tabular text into a worksheet are prerequisite skills for the MO-200 exam. This topic reviews procedures for importing delimited data from files.

See Also For more information about exam prerequisites, see this book's Introduction.

A delimited data file contains lines of data separated into a consistent field structure by using a character (the delimiter) to separate the field values. The delimiter can be any character, but the most common are the comma, tab, and colon. Delimited data can be saved in a plain-text (.txt) file or a comma-separated values (.csv) file. Delimited data files are supported by most database and spreadsheet applications and are commonly used when exporting data from a large database for import into another database application or an application such as Excel.

When you import delimited data from a file, Excel evaluates the file and displays a preview of the data as it will be imported. If the data exceeds certain size limits, the preview displays only a portion of the data and a message that it has been truncated due to size limits; however, this does not affect the amount of data that will be imported.

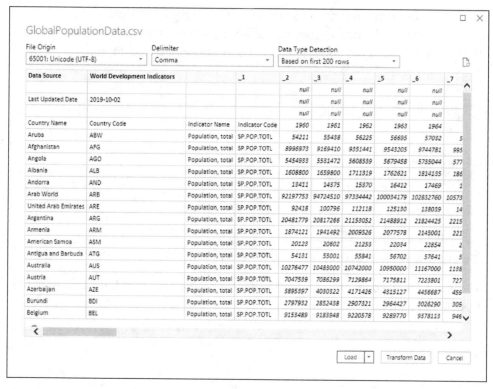

The import analysis for a CSV file containing global population data

◇◇

Exam Strategy The Text Import Wizard from earlier versions of Excel has been replaced by the Get Data tool, which offers more-advanced options but is also more difficult to use. If you aren't familiar with this tool, be sure to practice using it.

◇◇

Options for modifying the data import settings are in the lower-right corner of the preview window.

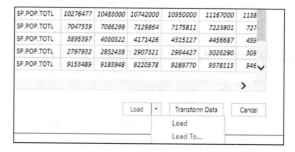

Select a data import location or modify data before importing it

The default import settings create a new worksheet in the open workbook. If you want to load the imported data to a specific worksheet, you can specify the worksheet and cell in which you want the upper-left corner of the imported data to start.

To import data into a specific location, you must specify it here

You can modify the data or import settings by using the data transform options in the Power Query Editor.

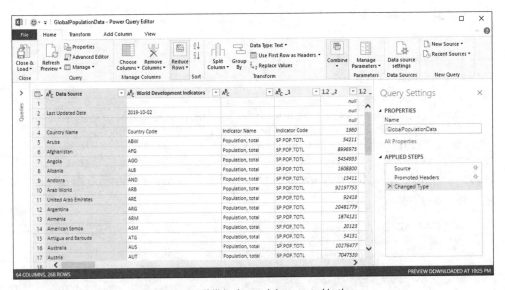

The Power Query Editor includes many capabilities beyond those tested in the exam

There are many ways to modify the data that will be imported from the source file. The most common modifications, and those that are likely to be tested in the MO-200 exam, are on the Home tab of the Power Query Editor ribbon. These include removing columns, removing blank rows, sorting data, and specifying whether the first row of data represents the column headers. (Alternatively, you can import the data as-is and make these changes in Excel.)

Changes you make in the Power Query Editor affect only the imported data, not the source file content.

To import the contents of a text (.txt) or comma-separated values (.csv) file

1. On the **Data** tab, in the **Get & Transform Data** group, do either of the following:

   - Click **From Text/CSV**.
   - Click **Get Data**, click **From File**, and then click **From Text/CSV**.

2. In the **Import Data** dialog box, browse to and select the delimited data file you want to import, and then click **Import**.

3. In the data import preview window, review the layout of the data as Excel plans to import it.

4. If the preview displays the data as you want to import it into the workbook, do either of the following:

   - To import the data into a new worksheet, click **Load**.
   - To import the data into an existing worksheet, click the **Load** arrow, and then click **Load To...** . In the **Import Data** dialog box that opens, select **Existing worksheet**, enter or select the cell in which you want the imported data to start, and then click **OK**.

5. If you want to modify the data before you import it, click **Transform Data** to open the Power Query Editor. Then follow any of the procedures described next.

To exclude columns from data during the import process

→ In the Power Query Editor, do either of the following:

   - Select the column or columns you want to remove, and then on the **Home** tab, in the **Manage Columns** group, click **Remove Columns**.
   - Select the column or columns you want to keep. On the **Home** tab, in the **Manage Columns** group, click the **Remove Columns** arrow, and then click **Remove Other Columns**.

To remove empty data rows

➔ In the Power Query Editor, do either of the following:

- Click the arrow to the right of any column header, and then on the **Home** tab, in the **Manage Columns** group, click **Remove Empty**.

- On the **Home** tab, in the **Manage Columns** group, click **Reduce Rows**, click **Remove Rows**, and then click **Remove Blank Rows**.

To sort data before importing it

➔ In the Power Query Editor, click the arrow to the right of the column header by which you want to sort, and then click **Sort Ascending** or **Sort Descending**:

To identify the column headers of a data set

1. In the Power Query Editor, display the top rows of the data set.

2. If the column headers above row 1 don't contain the column headings of the data set, identify the row (if any) that does.

3. If the data set does not contain column headings and the current headers are part of the data set, do the following:

   a. On the **Home** tab, in the **Transform** group, click the **Use First Row as Headers** arrow, and then click **Use Headers as First Row**.

   b. Follow the next procedure, "To rename column headers before importing data."

4. If the column headings are in row 1, on the **Home** tab, in the **Transform** group, click **Use First Row as Headers**.

5. If the column headings are in a row below row 1, do the following:

   a. On the **Home** tab, in the **Manage Columns** group, click **Reduce Rows**, click **Remove Rows**, and then click **Remove Top Rows**.

   b. In the **Remove Top Rows** dialog box, enter the number of data rows that are between the current column headers and the row you want to use as the column headers. Then click **OK**.

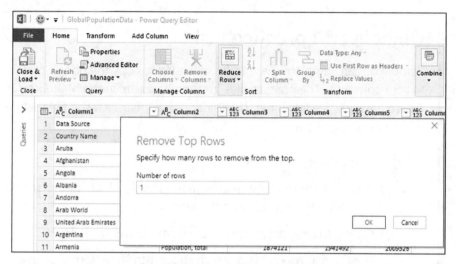

The command removes rows from the top of the data, not from the current location

   c. With the data you want to use as the column headers now in row 1, on the **Home** tab, in the **Transform** group, click **Use First Row as Headers**.

To rename column headers before importing data

1. In the Power Query Editor, right-click the column header you want to change, and then click **Rename**.

2. With the column name selected for editing, enter the name you want, and then press **Enter**.

To load data from the Power Query Editor to Excel

→ On the Home tab, in the Close group, do either of the following:

- To import the data into a new worksheet, click **Close & Load**.

- To import the data into an existing worksheet, click the **Close & Load** arrow, and then click **Close & Load To…** . In the **Import Data** dialog box that opens, select **Existing worksheet**, enter or select the cell in which you want the imported data to start, and then click **OK**.

Objective 1.1 practice tasks

Before you can complete these tasks, you need to copy the book's practice files to your computer. The practice files for these tasks are in the **MOSExcel2019\Objective1** practice file folder. The folder also contains a result file that you can use to check your work.

➤ Open the **Excel_1-1** workbook and do the following:

❑ Prepare to import the data from the **Excel_1-1_ContactList.txt** tab-delimited text file into the workbook.

❑ During the import process, transform the data as follows:

❑ Use the first row of data, which starts with "FirstName," as the column headers.

❑ Load the data into cell A4 of the Client Contacts worksheet.

➤ With the **Excel_1-1** workbook open, do the following:

❑ Prepare to import the data from the **Excel_1-1_GlobalPopulation.csv** file into the workbook.

❑ During the import process, transform the data as follows:

❑ Remove all blank rows from the data set.

❑ Use the row that starts with "Country Name" as the column header row.

❑ Remove the "Indicator Name" and "Indicator Code" columns from the data set.

❑ Load the data into a new worksheet.

➤ Save the **Excel_1-1** workbook and open the **Excel_1-1_results** workbook. Compare the two workbooks to check your work. Then close the open workbooks.

Objective 1.2: Navigate within workbooks

1

Search for data within a workbook

You can easily locate specific values, formula content, comment text, and formatting anywhere within a workbook. Using the Find operation, you can search the entire workbook or a specific worksheet for text and formatting in formulas, calculated values, or comments.

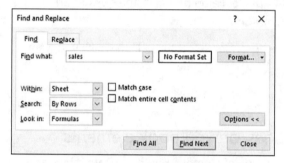

You can search a single worksheet or an entire workbook

To display the Find tab of the Find And Replace dialog box

→ On the **Home** tab, in the **Editing** group, click **Find & Select** to display the list, and then click **Find.**

→ Press **Ctrl+F**.

To search for text

1. Display the **Find** tab of the **Find and Replace** dialog box.

2. In the **Find what** box, enter the text you want to locate.

3. If the Options section is not expanded, click **Options** to display the search parameters, and then specify any of the following parameters:

   • In the **Within** list, click **Sheet** or **Workbook**.

   • In the **Search** list, click **By Rows** or **By Columns**.

   • In the **Look in** list, click **Formulas**, **Values**, or **Comments**.

   • Select the **Match case** or **Match entire cell contents** check boxes to further restrict your search.

4. Click **Find Next**.

To search for formatting

1. On the **Find** tab of the **Find and Replace** dialog box, click the **Format** button.

2. In the **Find Format** dialog box, specify the number, alignment, font, border, fill, or protection formatting you want to find. Then click **OK**.

3. In the **Find and Replace** dialog box, click **Find Next**.

To search for matching formatting

1. On the **Find** tab of the **Find and Replace** dialog box, click the **Format** arrow, and then click **Choose Format From Cell**.

2. When the pointer changes to an eyedropper, select the cell on which you want to base your search.

3. In the **Find and Replace** dialog box, click **Find Next**.

Navigate to named cells, ranges, or workbook elements

If you're looking for a specific element or type of element, you can locate it by using the Go To and Go To Special commands. From the Go To dialog box, you can locate any named element (such as a cell, cell range, named range, table, or chart). From the Go To Special dialog box, you can locate comments, formulas or specific formula elements, blank cells, objects, row or column differences, precedents and dependents, conditional formatting, data validation, and more.

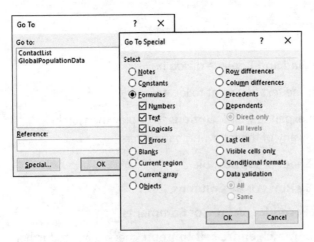

Move directly to specific workbook elements

To open the Go To dialog box

→ On the **Home** tab, in the **Editing** group, display the **Find & Select** list, and then click **Go To**.

To open the Go To Special dialog box

→ On the **Home** tab, in the **Editing** group, display the **Find & Select** list, and then click **Go To Special**.

→ Open the **Go To** dialog box, and then click the **Special** button.

To move to a named cell, range, or workbook element

→ On the formula bar, click the **Name** box arrow, and then select the named element.

→ Open the **Go To** dialog box. Click a named element in the **Go to** list, and then click **OK**.

To move to a location that has a specific property

1. Open the **Go To Special** dialog box.

2. In the **Select** area, click the property for which you want to search. Then click **OK**.

Insert and remove hyperlinks

Excel worksheets can include hyperlinks that provide a quick way to connect to related information or to create a pre-addressed email message. You can create a hyperlink from any cell to another location in the worksheet, in the workbook, in an external document, or on the web—any of the hyperlink locations supported by the Office 2019 programs.

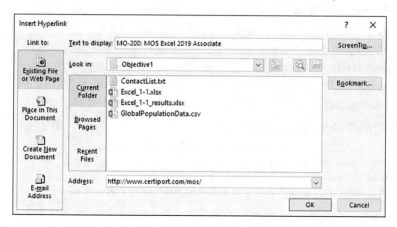

Link directly to another cell in the workbook

By default, hyperlinks are formatted as underlined, colored text. (The active and followed hyperlink colors are specified by the theme.) Clicking the hyperlink text in the cell that contains the hyperlink displays the hyperlink target.

Tip To select a cell that contains a hyperlink, click part of the cell away from the hyperlink, click and hold down the mouse button until the pointer changes to a plus sign and then click the cell, or click an adjacent cell and use the arrow keys to move to the cell that contains the hyperlink.

To open the Insert Hyperlink dialog box

→ Select the cell from which you want to hyperlink and then do either of the following:

- On the **Insert** tab, in the **Links** group, click the **Link** button (not the arrow).
- Press **Ctrl+K**.

To create a hyperlink to a webpage

→ Enter a URL in the cell, and then press **Enter**.

Or

1. Select the cell or object you want to link from.

2. Open the **Insert Hyperlink** dialog box.

3. In the **Link to** list, click **Existing File or Web Page**. Then do either of the following:

   - In the **Address** box, enter the URL of the webpage you want to link to.
   - Click the **Browse the Web** button (the button labeled with a globe and magnifying glass). In the web browser window that opens (not a previously opened window), display the webpage you want to link to. Move the window aside, if necessary, and click the **Insert Hyperlink** dialog box to copy the webpage address from the browser address bar to the **Address** box of the dialog box. Then minimize or close the browser window.

4. In the **Insert Hyperlink** dialog box, click **OK**.

Tip While inserting a hyperlink from a cell that contains text (not numeric data), the Text To Display box is active and displays the cell content. (Otherwise, it displays <<Selection in Document>>.) You can change the text in the cell by entering alternative text in the Text To Display box.

To link to an existing file or folder

1. Select the cell or object you want to link from.

2. Open the **Insert Hyperlink** dialog box.

3. In the **Link to** list, click **Existing File or Web Page**.

4. In the **Look in** area, browse to the file you want to link to, and double-click it to enter the file path and name in the Address box.

5. Click **OK**.

To create and link to an Excel workbook

1. Select the cell or object you want to link from, and then open the **Insert Hyperlink** dialog box.

2. In the **Link to** list, click **Create New Document**. Then review the location shown in the **Full path** section.

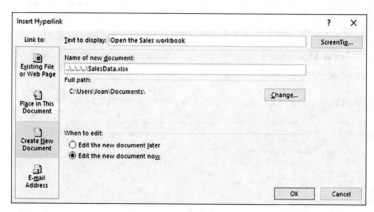

Simultaneously create a file and a link to it

3. If you want to create the new workbook in the folder shown in the **Full path** section, enter a name for the workbook in the **Name of new document** box. It is not necessary to append a file type extension.

   Or, if you want to create the new workbook in a different folder, do the following:

   a. Click the **Change** button.

   b. In the **Create New Document** dialog box, browse to the folder in which you want to save the file.

   c. In the **File Name** box, enter a name for the workbook, and append **.xlsx** to the workbook name to indicate the specific type of file you want to create. Then click **OK**.

4. In the **When to edit** area, do either of the following:

- To create a blank workbook in the folder but not open it, select **Edit the new document later**.

- To create a workbook and open it for editing, select **Edit the new document now**.

5. In the **Insert Hyperlink** dialog box, click **OK**.

6. If you chose the option to edit the workbook immediately, it opens now. Modify the file content as appropriate for the purposes of the hyperlink, and then save and close the file.

To create and link to a file of another type

1. Select the cell or object you want to link from, and then open the **Insert Hyperlink** dialog box.

2. In the **Link to** list, click **Create New Document**.

3. In the **Full path** section, click the **Change** button.

4. In the **Create New Document** dialog box, browse to the folder in which you want to create the file.

5. In the **Save as type** list, click the category of file you want to create.

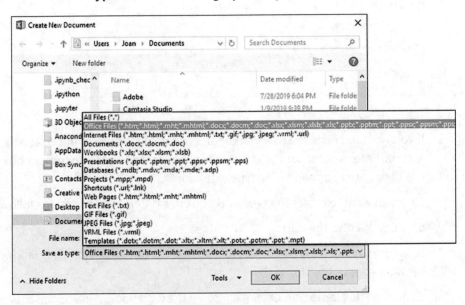

You can create and link to a wide variety of files

6. In the **File Name** box, enter a name and file extension for the new file.

7. In the **Create New Document** dialog box, click **OK**.

8. In the **When to edit** area of the **Insert Hyperlink** dialog box, click **Edit the new document later** or **Edit the new document now**.

9. In the **Insert Hyperlink** dialog box, click **OK**.

10. If you chose the option to edit the file immediately, it opens now. Modify the file content as appropriate for the purposes of the hyperlink, and then save and close the file.

To link to a cell, worksheet, or named object in the workbook

1. Select the cell or object you want to link from, and then open the **Insert Hyperlink** dialog box.

2. In the **Link to** list, click **Place in This Document**.

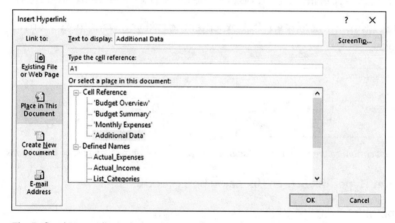

The Defined Names list includes objects such as tables and named data ranges

3. Do one of the following:

   - In the **Type the cell reference** box, enter a cell on the current worksheet or the path to a cell on another worksheet in the format *'WorksheetName'!A1*.

   - In the **Or select a place in this document** box, expand the **Cell Reference** list and click the worksheet you want to link to.

   - In the **Or select a place in this document** box, expand the **Defined Names** list and click the named object you want to link to.

4. In the **Insert Hyperlink** dialog box, click **OK**.

To create a hyperlink that creates a pre-addressed email message

1. Select the cell or object you want to link from, and then open the Insert Hyperlink dialog box.

2. In the **Insert Hyperlink** dialog box, in the **Link to** list, click **E-mail Address**.

3. Do either of the following:

    - In the **E-mail address** box, enter the email address of the message recipient.

    - In the **Recently used e-mail addresses** list, click an email address that you want to reuse.

4. In the **Subject** box, enter the message subject.

5. In the **Insert Hyperlink** dialog box, click **OK**.

To display alternative text when a user points to a hyperlink

1. In the **Insert Hyperlink** dialog box for the link, click the **ScreenTip** button.

2. In the **Set Hyperlink ScreenTip** box, enter the text you want the ScreenTip to display.

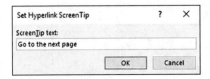

If you don't customize the ScreenTip, it displays the hyperlink destination and usage instructions

3. In the **Set Hyperlink ScreenTip** dialog box, click **OK**.

To edit a hyperlink

1. Right-click the hyperlink, and then click **Edit Hyperlink**.

2. In the **Edit Hyperlink** dialog box, modify any aspect of the hyperlink. Then click **OK**.

To remove a hyperlink

- Right-click the hyperlink, and then click **Remove Hyperlink**.

Objective 1.2 practice tasks

The practice file for these tasks is in the **MOSExcel2019\Objective1** practice file folder. The folder also contains a result file that you can use to check your work.

➤ Open the **Excel_1-2** workbook and do the following:

☐ Search the workbook for all instances of the word *garden*. Confirm that the search returns results from both worksheets.

☐ Search the workbook for text formatted with a White font color. Change the font color to Orange to show that you found it.

➤ Display the **Product List** worksheet and do the following:

☐ Move to the first cell that contains a comment.

☐ Move to the cell range named *berry_bushes*.

☐ Move to cell F13.

☐ Create a hyperlink from cell F13 to the *berry_bushes* cell range.

☐ Move to the cell at the intersection of the last active row and column in the worksheet.

➤ Display the **Employees** worksheet and do the following:

☐ In cell C12, enter a hyperlink to the website located at **www.adventure-works.com**.

☐ Edit the hyperlink so that the cell displays *Please visit our website* instead of the URL.

➤ Save the **Excel_1-2** workbook and open the **Excel_1-2_results** workbook. Compare the two workbooks to check your work. Then close the open workbooks.

Objective 1.3: Format worksheets and workbooks

Modify page setup

You can control the basic footprint of printed worksheets by defining the page size and orientation, changing the page margins, and changing the space allocated to the header and footer. By configuring these page setup options, you define the space that is available for the content on an individual page when it is printed or displayed in Print Layout view.

Tip If your content doesn't fit within the allocated area, you can adjust the way it fits on the page by scaling it. For more information, see "Objective 1.5: Configure content for collaboration."

To set a standard page size

→ On the **Page Layout** tab, in the **Page Setup** group, click the **Size** button, and then click the paper size you want.

To set a custom page size

1. On the **Page Layout** tab, in the **Page Setup** group, click the **Size** button, and then click **More Paper Sizes**.

2. On the **Page** tab of the **Page Setup** dialog box, click **Options**.

3. On the **Paper/Quality** tab of the **Printer Properties** dialog box, in the **Paper Options** area, click **Custom**.

4. In the **Custom Paper Size** dialog box, enter a name for the custom size, enter the width and length of the paper, specify the units of measurement, click **Save**, and then click **Close**.

5. Click **OK** in each of the open dialog boxes.

Tip The available print settings depend on the currently selected printer.

To change the page margins

1. On the **Page Layout** tab, in the **Page Setup** group, click the **Margins** button.

2. On the **Margins** menu, do either of the following:

   • Click the standard margin setting you want.

- Click the **Custom Margins** command. Then on the **Margins** tab of the **Page Setup** dialog box, specify the **Top**, **Bottom**, **Left**, and **Right** margins, and click **OK**.

To change the page orientation

→ On the **Page Layout** tab, in the **Page Setup** group, click the **Orientation** button, and then click **Portrait** or **Landscape**.

Adjust row height and column width

An Excel 2019 worksheet can contain up to 1,048,576 rows and 16,384 columns of data. When you insert or delete rows and columns, you change the data structure on the worksheet rather than the worksheet itself. Inserting a row or column within a data range or table shifts existing content down or to the right; deleting a row or column shifts content up or to the left. Excel tidily updates any cell references within formulas to reflect the row and column changes.

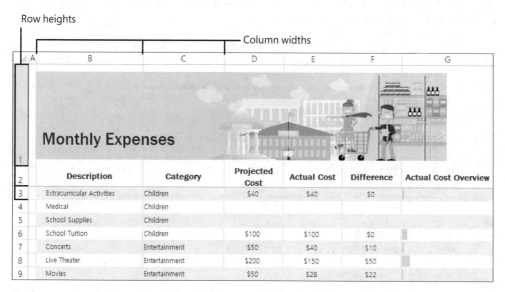

Configure rows and columns to fit their contents

By default, Excel 2019 worksheet rows have a standard height of 15 points, or 0.21 inches, and their height increases and decreases to accommodate the number of lines in their longest entry, up to a maximum of 409 points. You can manually change the height of a row, but it is best to leave the row height dynamic to accommodate future changes, unless you have a good reason to specify a height. For example, you might want to specify a narrow row to create a visual break between blocks of data. (You can restore dynamic height adjustment if needed.)

Worksheet columns have a standard width of 8.43 characters (in the default font), or 0.72 inches, and their width is not dynamic. You are more likely to want to change column width than row height, usually to accommodate long cell entries. You can have Excel adjust a column to fit its longest entry, or you can adjust it manually to up to 255 characters. In conjunction with text wrapping, adjusting column widths is a key technique for making as much data as possible visible on the screen or page.

Tip In Normal view, row heights are specified in points and column widths are specified in characters. In Page Layout view, row heights and column widths are specified in inches (or your default unit of measure).

For the purposes of height and width adjustments, selecting a single cell in a row or column is the same as selecting the entire row or column. You can change the height or width of multiple rows or columns at the same time by selecting them and then performing the resizing operation.

See Also For information about inserting individual cells, see "Objective 2.1: Manipulate data in worksheets."

To change the height of one or more rows

→ Drag the bottom border of the row selector up or down.

Tip As you drag the border, a ScreenTip displays the current row height in either points or inches and in pixels.

Or

1. Select the row or rows you want to change.

2. Do either of the following:

   - Right-click the selection, and then click **Row Height**.

   - On the **Home** tab, in the **Cells** group, click **Format** to display the list, and then click **Row Height**.

3. In the **Row Height** dialog box, specify the height you want, and then click **OK**.

To change the width of a column

→ Drag the right border of the column selector to the left or right.

> **Tip** As you drag the border, a ScreenTip displays the current column width in either characters or inches and in pixels.

Or

1. Select the column or columns whose width you want to change.

2. Do either of the following:

   • Right-click the selection, and then click **Column Width**.

   • On the **Home** tab, in the **Cells** group, display the **Format** list, and then click **Column Width**.

3. In the **Column Width** dialog box, specify the width you want, and then click **OK**.

To size a column or row to fit its contents

→ Double-click the right border of the column heading or the bottom border of the row heading.

→ Select the column. On the **Home** tab, in the **Cells** group, display the **Format** list, and then click **AutoFit Column Width**.

→ Select the row. On the **Home** tab, in the **Cells** group, display the **Format** list, and then click **AutoFit Row Height**.

> **Tip** You can adjust the width of all the columns in a worksheet at the same time. Click the worksheet selector to select the entire worksheet, and then double-click the border between any two columns. Every populated column resizes to fit its contents. Empty columns remain unchanged.

Customize headers and footers

You can display information on every page of a printed worksheet, and in Page Layout view, by inserting it in the page headers and footers. You can have a different header and footer on the first page or different headers and footers on odd and even pages. When you create a header or footer, Excel displays the workbook in a view similar to Page Layout view, and the Design tool tab appears on the ribbon.

An active header or footer is divided into three sections. You can insert content directly into the worksheet header sections or build the content in the Header dialog box.

You can enter document information and properties such as the current or total page number, current date or time, file path, file name, or sheet name from the Design tool tab, or you can enter and format text the same way you would in the worksheet body. You can also insert an image, such as a company logo.

To insert a standard header or footer

1. On the **Page Layout** tab, in the **Page Setup** group, click the dialog box launcher.

2. In the **Page Setup** dialog box, click the **Header/Footer** tab.

3. In the **Header** list or **Footer** list, click the content you want to display in that area.

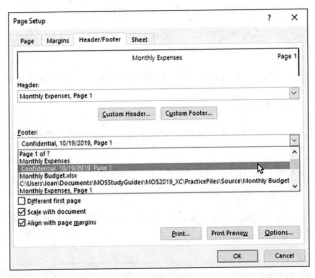

Select from standard document properties or create a custom entry

4. In the **Page Setup** dialog box, click **OK**.

Tip You can't format header or footer text from within the Page Setup dialog box, but you can insert the content and then format it in Page Layout view.

To build a custom header or footer

1. On the **Header/Footer** tab of the **Page Setup** dialog box, click the **Custom Header** or **Custom Footer** button.

2. Click the left, center, or right box to edit the corresponding section of the header or footer.

3. Do any of the following:

- Insert text, then select the text and click the **Format Text** button to change the font formatting.

- Click the buttons to insert document properties such as page number, number of pages, date, time, file path, file name, and worksheet name.

- Click the **Insert Picture** button to insert a local or online image.

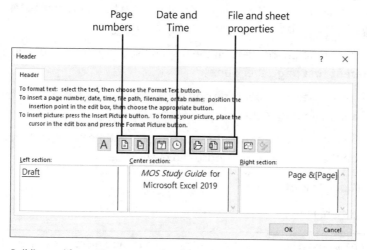

Building and formatting a custom header

4. When you finish, click **OK** in the **Header** or **Footer** dialog box and in the **Page Setup** dialog box.

To activate the page header area of the worksheet

→ In **Normal** view, on the **Insert** tab, in the **Text** group, click **Header & Footer**.

→ In **Page Layout** view, at the top of the page, click **Add header**.

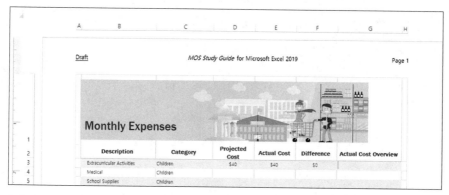

In Page Layout view, you can enter header and footer elements directly onto the worksheet

To activate the page footer area of the worksheet

→ In **Normal** view, on the **Insert** tab, in the **Text** group, click **Header & Footer**. Then on the **Design** tool tab, click **Go to Footer**.

→ In **Page Layout** view, at the bottom of the page, click **Add footer**.

To configure header or footer options

1. In the **Options** group on the **Design** tool tab, or on the **Header/Footer** tab of the **Page Setup** dialog box, do either of the following:

   - To display different headers on the first and subsequent pages, select the **Different first page** check box.

   - To display different headers on odd and even pages, select the **Different odd and even pages** check box.

2. Review the page headers and footers and ensure that the correct information appears on the first, subsequent, odd, and even pages.

To close the header or footer area

→ Click anywhere in the worksheet body.

Tip If you decide to insert a header or footer just before printing, you can do so from the Header/Footer tab of the Page Setup dialog box, which is accessible from the Print page of the Backstage view.

To edit the header or footer

→ Activate the header or footer, and then make your changes.

Objective 1.3 practice tasks

The practice file for these tasks is in the **MOSExcel2019\Objective1** practice file folder. The folder also contains a result file that you can use to check your work.

➤ Open the **Excel_1-3** workbook and do the following:

➤ Display the *Period1* worksheet and do the following:

❑ Configure the worksheet to print at a Landscape orientation. Display the print preview of the worksheet to verify the settings.

❑ Create a header that will print on all pages of the worksheet. In the left header section, enter the Current Date property; in the center section, enter the File Name property; and in the right section, enter the Page Number property.

❑ Change the center section of the header to display the name of the worksheet instead of the workbook.

➤ Display the *Period2* worksheet and do the following:

❑ Resize columns D:O to fit their content.

❑ Check the width of column D, and then set column C to the same width.

➤ Save the **Excel_1-3** workbook.

➤ Open the **Excel_1-3_results** workbook. Compare the two workbooks to check your work. Then close the open workbooks.

Objective 1.4: Customize options and views

Customize the Quick Access Toolbar

By default, buttons representing the Save, Undo, and Redo commands (as well as the AutoSave command, which is active when the file is in a shared location, and the Touch/Mouse Mode command, when you're working on a touchscreen device) appear on the Quick Access Toolbar in the Excel program window. If you regularly use a few commands that are scattered on various tabs of the ribbon and you don't want to switch between tabs to access the commands, you can add them to the Quick Access Toolbar so that they're always available to you. You can add commands to the Quick Access Toolbar from the Customize Quick Access Toolbar menu (which includes eight additional common commands), from the ribbon, or from the Excel Options dialog box. You can add any type of command to the Quick Access Toolbar, even a drop-down list of options or a gallery of thumbnails.

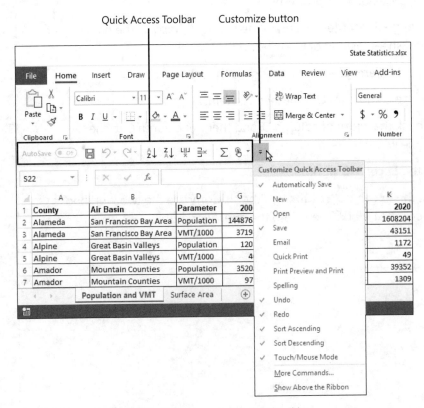

The Quick Access Toolbar with custom commands, below the ribbon

You save time by placing frequently used commands on the Quick Access Toolbar. To save even more time, you can move the Quick Access Toolbar from its default position above the ribbon to below the ribbon, so your mouse has less distance to travel from the content you're working with to the command you want to invoke. If you add all the buttons you use most often to the Quick Access Toolbar, you can hide the ribbon to gain screen space.

You can modify the Quick Access Toolbar by adding, moving, separating, or removing commands. You can add commands in several ways, but you can modify and separate commands only from the Excel Options dialog box. From that dialog box, you can modify the Quick Access Toolbar that appears in the program window or create a custom Quick Access Toolbar that appears only in the currently active workbook.

To display the Quick Access Toolbar page of the Excel Options dialog box

→ Right-click a blank area of the ribbon, and then click **Customize Quick Access Toolbar**.

→ Click the **Customize Quick Access Toolbar** button, and then click **More Commands**.

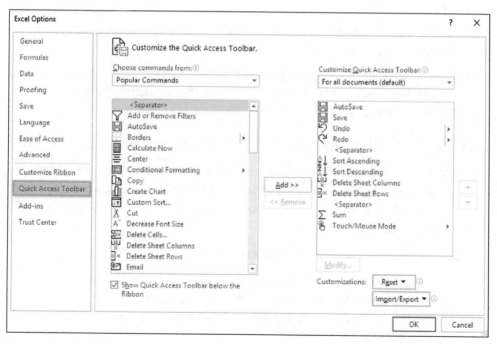

You can customize the Quick Access Toolbar for all workbooks or create one unique to the current workbook

To add commands to the Quick Access Toolbar

→ Click the **Customize Quick Access Toolbar** button, and then click one of the common commands displayed on the menu.

→ Right-click a command on the ribbon, and then click **Add to Quick Access Toolbar**.

Or

1. Display the **Quick Access Toolbar** page of the **Excel Options** dialog box.

2. In the **Choose commands from** list, click the group of commands from which you want to select.

3. In the **Choose commands** pane, locate the command you want to add, and then click the **Add** button.

4. In the **Excel Options** dialog box, click **OK**.

To remove a command from the Quick Access Toolbar

→ Right-click the command on the **Quick Access Toolbar**, and then click **Remove from Quick Access Toolbar**.

→ On the **Customize Quick Access Toolbar** menu, click any active command (indicated by a check mark) to remove it.

→ On the **Quick Access Toolbar** page of the **Excel Options** dialog box, in the **Customize Quick Access Toolbar** pane, click the command. Then click the **Remove** button.

To change the order of commands on the Quick Access Toolbar

→ On the **Quick Access Toolbar** page of the **Excel Options** dialog box, in the **Customize Quick Access Toolbar** pane, click the command you want to move. Then click **Move Up** to move the command to the left or **Move Down** to move it to the right.

To separate commands on the Quick Access Toolbar

→ On the **Quick Access Toolbar** page of the **Excel Options** dialog box, in the **Customize Quick Access Toolbar** pane, click the command after which you want to insert a separator. At the top of the **Choose commands** pane, click **<Separator>**. Then click **Add**.

To create a Quick Access Toolbar that is specific to the current workbook

→ On the **Quick Access Toolbar** page of the **Excel Options** dialog box, in the **Customize Quick Access Toolbar** list, click **For** *document name*. Then add buttons to the toolbar as usual.

To change the location of the Quick Access Toolbar

→ On the **Customize Quick Access Toolbar** menu, click **Show Below the Ribbon** or **Show Above the Ribbon**.

→ Right-click the **Quick Access Toolbar**, and then click **Show Quick Access Toolbar Below the Ribbon** or **Show Quick Access Toolbar Above the Ribbon**.

→ On the **Quick Access Toolbar** page of the **Excel Options** dialog box, select or clear the **Show Quick Access Toolbar below the Ribbon** check box.

To reset the Quick Access Toolbar to its default content

→ On the **Quick Access Toolbar** page of the **Excel Options** dialog box, click the **Reset** button, and then click **Reset only Quick Access Toolbar** or **Reset all customizations**.

Tip Resetting the Quick Access Toolbar doesn't change its location.

Modify the display of content

Display worksheet content in different views

From the View toolbar at the bottom of the program window, or from the View tab, you can switch among three views of a worksheet:

- **Normal** The worksheet is displayed in the window at 100 percent magnification or the zoom level you select. Page breaks are indicated by black dashed lines.

- **Page Break Preview** The entire worksheet is displayed in the window, with page breaks indicated by bold blue dashed lines and page numbers displayed in the center of each page. You can change the page breaks by dragging the blue lines.

- **Page Layout** Each worksheet page is displayed on the screen as it will be printed, with space between the individual pages. If the display of rulers is on, rulers appear on the top and left edges of the window. The page header and footer are visible, and you can select them for editing.

Buttons for changing the view are located on the View tab of the ribbon and on the View Shortcuts toolbar near the right end of the status bar.

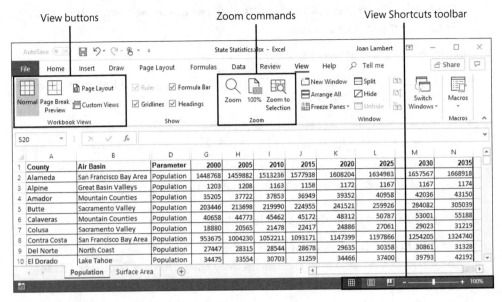

View and Zoom commands on the toolbar and status bar

To change the worksheet view

→ On the **View** tab, in the **Workbook Views** group, click the **Normal**, **Page Layout**, or **Page Break Preview** button.

→ On the **View Shortcuts** toolbar near the right end of the status bar, click the **Normal**, **Page Layout**, or **Page Break Preview** button.

Freeze worksheet rows and columns

It can be cumbersome to work in a worksheet that is too long or wide to display legibly in the program window, to scroll up and down or back and forth to view data elsewhere in the worksheet, or to switch back and forth between multiple worksheets in the same workbook if you frequently need to access information in both of them.

You can view multiple parts of a worksheet at one time by freezing rows or columns so they stay in view while you scroll the rest of the worksheet, by splitting the window so you can independently scroll and work in two or four views of the worksheet within the same program window, or by displaying multiple instances of the workbook in separate program windows. Regardless of the technique you use, changes you make to the workbook content in any one view are immediately reflected in the others.

Tip Another way to display disparate rows or columns together on one screen is to hide the rows or columns between them.

To freeze the first row or column of a worksheet

→ On the **View** tab, in the **Window** group, click the **Freeze Panes** button, and then click **Freeze Top Row** or **Freeze First Column**.

To freeze multiple rows or columns

1. Select the row below or column to the right of those you want to freeze, by clicking the row selector or column selector.

2. On the **View** tab, in the **Window** group, click the **Freeze Panes** button, and then click **Freeze Panes**.

To simultaneously freeze columns and rows

1. Select the cell that is below and to the right of the intersection of the row and column you want to freeze.

2. On the **View** tab, in the **Window** group, click the **Freeze Panes** button, and then click **Freeze Panes**.

Tip You can freeze as many columns and rows as you like depending on what cell is selected when you invoke the Freeze Panes command. Selecting a cell in row 1 freezes the columns to the left of that cell. Selecting a cell in column A freezes the rows above that cell. Selecting cell A1 freezes the panes at the midpoint of the current window (the top half of the rows and the left half of the columns). Selecting a cell other than those in row 1 and column A freezes the rows above and columns to the left of the cell.

To unfreeze all rows and columns

→ On the **View** tab, in the **Window** group, click the **Freeze Panes** button, and then click **Unfreeze Panes**.

Display multiple parts of a worksheet

To split a worksheet in the program window

1. Do either of the following:

   - To split the window into two parts, click a cell in row 1 or column A.
   - To split the window into four parts, click the cell that you want to designate as the inside corner of the lower-right quadrant.

2. On the **View** tab, in the **Window** group, click **Split**.

To modify the split between windows

→ Drag the vertical or horizontal split bar to the row or column where you want to split the window.

To remove a split from a program window

→ Double-click a split bar to remove it.

→ Drag a vertical split bar to the top of the scroll bar to remove it.

→ Drag a horizontal split bar to the right end of the scroll bar to remove it.

→ On the **View** toolbar, click the active **Split** button to remove all splits.

Display multiple parts of a workbook

To display multiple views of a workbook in separate program windows

1. On the **View** tab, in the **Window** group, click the **New Window** button to open another instance of the workbook.

   Tip You can open several instances of the workbook; Excel displays the instance number after the workbook name in the program window title bar.

   ---

2. Arrange the workbook windows as you want or click the **Arrange All** button and then in the **Arrange Windows** dialog box, click **Tiled**, **Horizontal**, **Vertical**, or **Cascade**. To arrange only the instances of the active workbook, select the **Windows of active workbook** check box. Then click **OK**.

3. Display the worksheet, worksheet section, or workbook element you want in each workbook window.

4. To return to a single program window, close the others. It is not necessary to save changes in any but the last open instance of the workbook.

Display formulas

Many worksheets contain formulas for the purpose of calculating data. A formula is visible in the formula bar when you click the cell that contains it, but its resulting value is visible in the cell. If you need to review multiple formulas, it is easier to do so if you first display them.

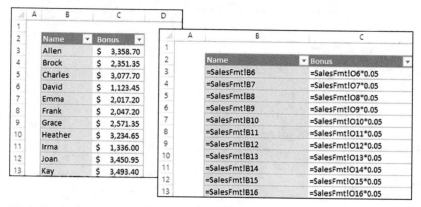

Displaying the formulas behind worksheet values

To display all formulas in a worksheet

➜ On the **Formulas** tab, in the **Formula Auditing** group, click the **Show Formulas** button.

To display the formula in the currently selected cell(s)

➜ Press **Ctrl+'**.

Modify basic workbook properties

Before distributing a workbook, you might want to attach properties to it so that the file is readily identifiable in the Details view of any browsing dialog box, such as the Open dialog box. In Excel 2019, workbook properties are easily accessible from the Info page of the Backstage view. By default, the Properties area of the Info page displays some automatically tracked properties such as the file size, the creation and last modification dates, and the people who created and last modified the file, as well as optional properties such as the file title, tags, and categories. You can expand the Properties shown on the Info page to include comments, status, subject, and other optional properties. You can access even more properties and create custom proper-ties from the file's Properties dialog box, which you can open from the Info page or from File Explorer.

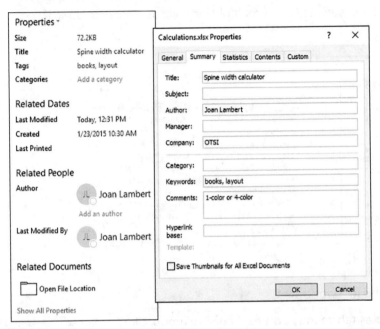

Workbook properties can be used to locate a workbook in File Explorer or on a SharePoint site

You can view and modify some properties directly on the Info page, or you can work in the Properties dialog box.

To set or change a basic property

➔ On the **Info** page of the Backstage view, click the property to activate it, and then add or change information.

To display additional common properties

➔ On the **Info** page of the Backstage view, click **Show All Properties**.

To display all properties in the Properties dialog box

➔ On the **Info** page of the Backstage view, click **Properties**, and then click **Advanced Properties**.

➔ In File Explorer, right-click the file, and then click **Properties**.

Objective 1.4 practice tasks

The practice file for these tasks is in the **MOSExcel2019\Objective1** practice file folder. The folder also contains a result file that you can use to check your work.

➤ Open the **Excel_1-4** workbook, display the **Inventory List** worksheet, and do the following:

❑ Add the Calculator button (which is not available on any ribbon tab) to the Quick Access Toolbar. Make it the leftmost button and insert a separator between it and the other buttons.

❑ Create a Quick Access Toolbar for the current workbook only. Add the Insert Combo Chart, Insert Picture, and Insert Table buttons (all available on the Insert tab). Then display the Quick Access Toolbar below the ribbon.

➤ Display the **My Monthly Budget** worksheet and do the following:

❑ Freeze rows 1 through 9 so that when you scroll the rest of the worksheet, those rows are always visible.

❑ Split the worksheet so that you can display rows 1 through 9 in the top window and scroll the budget data in the bottom window.

❑ Attach the keywords (tags) *spending* and *saving* to the workbook.

❑ Display the **My Monthly Budget** worksheet in Page Layout view.

❑ Select the *Projected Monthly Income* section of the worksheet and zoom in to display only the selected cells.

❑ Display the formulas behind the data on the worksheet.

➤ Save the **Excel_1-4** workbook and open the **Excel_1-4_results** workbook. Compare the two workbooks to check your work. Then close the open workbooks.

Objective 1.5: Configure content for collaboration

Inspect workbooks for issues

Excel includes three tools that you can use to inspect a workbook for possible problems before you distribute it electronically (as a file): the Document Inspector, the Accessibility Checker, and the Compatibility Checker.

Inspect a workbook for hidden properties or personal information

The Document Inspector checks for content and information that you might not want to share with readers, such as:

- Information that identifies the document author and aspects of the workbook and the computer system on which the workbook is stored

- Comments and ink annotations

- Page headers and footers

- Data that isn't visible, including hidden worksheets, rows, columns, and names; filtered data; and objects that have been formatted as invisible

- PivotTables, PivotCharts, cube formulas, slicers, and timelines that might reference hidden data

- Embedded files, file links, and data from external sources

- Content add-ins and Task Pane add-ins that are saved in the workbook

- Real-time data functions that can pull external data into the workbook

- Excel Survey questions, defined scenarios

- Macros, form controls, and ActiveX controls saved as part of the workbook

The Document Inspector offers to remove some types of content and alerts you to other types of content that it can't remove—you would need to review and modify these manually. You can opt to remove or retain any category of content. There are some types of content that you might want to keep and review individually.

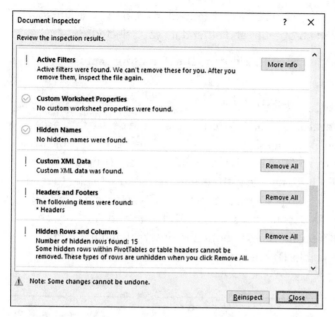

Some of the results reported by the Document Inspector

To inspect a workbook for common issues

1. Save the workbook, and then display the **Info** page of the Backstage view.

2. In the **Inspect Workbook** area of the **Info** page, click the **Check for Issues** button, and then click **Inspect Document** to open the Document Inspector dialog box, which lists the items that will be checked.

3. Clear the check boxes for any groups of properties you don't want to check for, and then click **Inspect** to display a report on the presence of the properties you selected.

4. Review the results, and then click the **Remove All** button for any category of information that you want the Document Inspector to remove for you.

    Some types of content, such as hidden names, display a More Info button instead of a Remove All button. The Document Inspector can't remove these content types for you; clicking the More Info button opens a webpage that provides information that will help you locate the content.

    Tip You can choose to retain content identified by the Document Inspector if you know that it is appropriate for distribution.

1

5. In the **Document Inspector** dialog box, click **Reinspect**, and then click **Inspect** to verify the removal of the properties and other data you selected.

6. When you're satisfied with the results, close the **Document Inspector** dialog box.

Inspect a workbook for accessibility issues

Accessible content is equally available to people regardless of the device they access it on and any visual or auditory disabilities. The Accessibility Checker is available in Word, Excel, Outlook, OneNote, and PowerPoint to identify content structure and formatting that might be difficult for people with certain kinds of disabilities to read or for assistive devices such as screen readers to access. These issues are divided by decreasing severity into three classifications: Errors, Warnings, and Tips. In Excel workbooks, the Accessibility Checker inspects content to ensure that it meets the criteria shown in the following table. (There are no Tip-level accessibility rules for Excel content.)

Error rules	Warning rules
• All non-text content has alternative text • Tables specify column header information • An applied number format uses something other than text color to indicate negative numbers • Workbook access is not restricted	• Tables have simple structures without split or merged cells • Sheet tabs have meaningful names • Text and background colors have enough contrast

See Also For detailed information about these and other Accessibility Checker rules, go to *https://support.office.com/article/rules-for-the-accessibility-checker-651e08f2-0fc3-4e10-aaca-74b4a67101c1* (or go to *support.office.microsoft.com* and search for "Accessibility Checker rules"). For more information about designing documents for accessibility, display the Accessibility Checker pane, and then at the bottom of the pane, click Read More About Making Documents Accessible.

Running the Accessibility Checker displays a list of issues in the Accessibility Checker pane. You can select any issue to display information about why it might be a problem and how to fix it.

You can leave the Accessibility Checker pane open while you work—it automatically updates to indicate current issues.

The Accessibility Checker pane provides links to and solutions for the issues it detects

---

Tip After you run the Accessibility Checker, information about workbook content issues is also shown in the Inspect Workbook area of the Info page of the Backstage view.

To inspect a workbook for accessibility issues

1. On the **Info** page of the Backstage view, click the **Check for Issues** button, and then click **Check Accessibility** to run the Accessibility Checker.

2. In the **Accessibility Checker** pane, review the inspection results and make any changes you want to the workbook.

3. When you are done, do either of the following:

   - Click the **X** in the upper-right corner of the **Accessibility Checker** pane to close the pane.

   - Leave the pane open to continue checking for accessibility issues as you work with the workbook.

Inspect a workbook for compatibility issues

The Compatibility Checker identifies formatting and features that aren't supported or won't work as expected in Excel 2010 and earlier versions. Fixing these issues ensures that the appearance and functionality of the workbook will be consistent for all readers.

The Compatibility Checker has two categories of issues:

- **Significant loss of functionality** These issues will cause the workbook to lose data or functionality.

- **Minor loss of fidelity** The workbook might not look or work the same way when you open it in an earlier version of Excel.

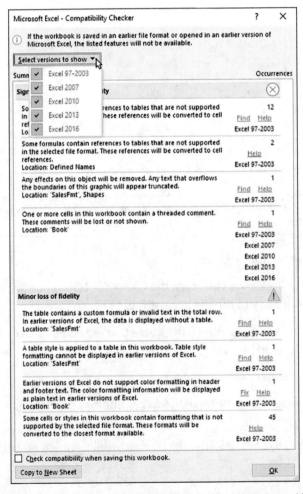

You can specify the versions of Excel with which you want the workbook to be compatible

The following table identifies worksheet content and features that aren't compatible with some earlier versions of Excel (notably Excel 97–2003).

Minor loss of fidelity	Significant loss of functionality
• Table style formatting • Color formatting in header and footer text • Even page or first page headers and footers • Unsupported cell formatting and style options (such as special effects and shadows) • More than 4,000 unique cell formatting combinations • More than 512 unique font formats	• Threaded comments (new in Excel 2019) • Sparklines and newer chart types such as treemaps • More than 256 columns or 65,536 rows of data, or data scenarios that reference cells outside these limits • Non-Gregorian calendar formats, such as Thai Buddhist, Arabic Hirji, or custom international formats • More than 64,000 cell blocks of data • Other features not supported prior to Excel 97–2003

To inspect a workbook for compatibility issues

1. On the **Info** page of the Backstage view, click the **Check for Issues** button, and then click **Check Compatibility**. The window immediately displays any formatting or features in the workbook that aren't compatible with Excel 97–2003, Excel 2007, Excel 2010, or Excel 2013.

2. To refine the list, click **Select versions to show** and then click Excel 97–2003, Excel 2007, Excel 2010, or Excel 2013 to select or clear the version from the compatibility requirements. Selected versions are indicated by check marks preceding the version.

To correct compatibility issues

1. Review the issue description and note the number of instances of the issue within the workbook. Some issues include a Help link to additional information.

2. Locate the named element by searching or scanning the worksheets, and then remove or modify it to meet the compatibility requirements.

3. When you finish, click **OK** to close the Compatibility Checker.

To maintain backward compatibility with a previous version of Excel

1. When saving the document, choose the previous file format in the **Save as type** list.

2. In the **Microsoft Excel - Compatibility Checker** window, click **Continue** to convert the unsupported features.

Print workbook content

An Excel workbook can contain many separate worksheets of data. You can print part or all of an individual worksheet, a selected worksheet, or all the worksheets that contain content at one time.

Print all or part of a workbook

By default, Excel prints only the currently active worksheet or worksheet group. You can choose specific print scopes from the Print page of the Backstage view.

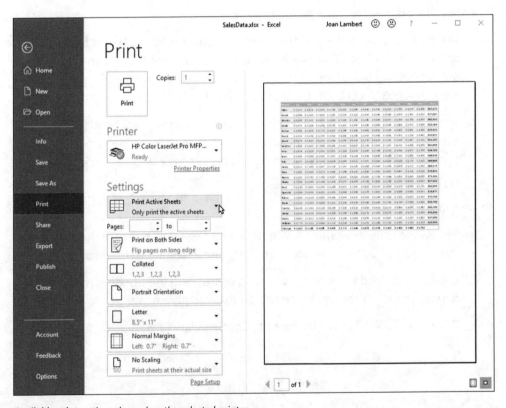

Available print settings depend on the selected printer

To print all populated worksheets in a workbook

➜ On the **Print** page of the Backstage view, in the **Settings** area, click **Print Entire Workbook** in the first list.

To print a single worksheet

1. Display the worksheet that you want to print.

2. On the **Print** page of the Backstage view, in the **Settings** area, click **Print Active Sheets** in the first list.

To print specific worksheets

1. Group the worksheets that you want to print.

2. On the **Print** page of the Backstage view, in the **Settings** area, click **Print Active Sheets** in the first list.

To print a portion of a worksheet

1. On the worksheet, select the range of cells you want to print.

2. On the **Print** page of the Backstage view, in the **Settings** area, click **Print Selection** in the first list.

Print all or part of a worksheet

If you want to print only part of a worksheet, you can do so from the Print page of the Backstage view as described in the previous topic. Alternatively, if you will often print the same portion of a worksheet, you can define that portion as the print area.

After defining the print area of a workbook, you can add selected ranges to it. A range that is contiguous to the original range becomes part of the original print area definition; a range that is noncontiguous or a different shape becomes a separate print area and is printed on a separate page. You can also remove ranges from the print area.

If you don't want to limit printing to the print area, you can permanently clear the print area, or you can temporarily ignore it when printing the worksheet.

To define a selected range as the print area

➜ On the **Page Layout** tab, in the **Page Setup** group, click the **Print Area** button, and then click **Set Print Area**.

To add a selected range to a defined print area

→ On the **Page Layout** tab, in the **Page Setup** group, click the **Print Area** button, and then click **Add to Print Area**.

Tip The Add To Print Area option is not displayed when the selected area of the worksheet is already part of the designated print area.

To remove a range from the print area

1. On the **Page Layout** tab, click the **Page Setup** dialog box launcher.

2. On the **Sheet** tab of the **Page Setup** dialog box, change the range reference in the **Print area** box, and then click **OK**.

To clear the print area

→ On the **Page Layout** tab, in the **Page Setup** group, click the **Print Area** button, and then click **Clear Print Area**.

To ignore the print area

→ On the **Print** page of the Backstage view, in the **Settings** area, click **Ignore Print Area** in the first list.

Tip The Ignore Print Area setting remains active (indicated by a check mark) until you turn it off by clicking it again.

Print sheet elements

When printing worksheet content, you have the option of printing some of the non-content elements that support the content, including the gridlines, row headings (the numbers on the left side of the sheet), column headings (the letters at the top of the sheet), comments, and cell error messages. Gridlines and row and column headings print as they look in the worksheet. You can choose to print comments in their actual locations or group them at the end of the sheet. You can print errors as they appear on the worksheet, delete them, or replace them with -- or #N/A.

If your worksheet contains multiple pages of tabular content, it will likely be helpful to readers to have the table column and row headings repeated on the top and left side of each page. You can designate the specific columns and rows to use for this purpose.

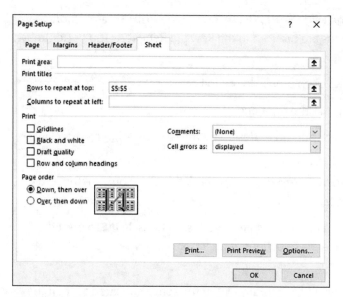

Options for printing supporting content and tabular content headers

To print supporting content

1. On the **Page Layout** tab, in the **Page Setup** group, click **Print Titles**.

2. On the **Sheet** tab of the **Page Setup** dialog box, in the **Print** section, do any of the following:

    *   Select the **Gridlines** check box to print the gridlines.

    *   Select the **Row and column headings** check box to print the row numbers and column letters.

    *   In the **Comments** list, click **At end of sheet** or **As displayed on sheet** to print cell comments in that location.

    *   In the **Cell errors as** list, click **displayed**, **--**, or **#N/A** to print the errors as specified, or click **<blank>** to hide the errors.

3. Click **Print Preview** to review the results of your selections, **Print** to print the worksheet, or **OK** to save the selections and return to the worksheet.

To display repeating row and column titles on multipage worksheets

1. In the worksheet, select the row(s) you want to repeat at the top of each page or the column(s) you want to repeat on the left side of each page.

2. On the **Page Layout** tab, in the **Page Setup** group, click **Print Titles**.

3. On the **Sheet** tab of the **Page Setup** dialog box, in the **Print titles** section, the selected rows or columns are prefilled in the Rows To Repeat At Top or Columns To Repeat At Left box.

4. To designate other rows or columns, do the following:

   a. Click the cell selector at the right end of the box.

   b. In the worksheet, click or drag to designate the rows or columns you want to include.

   c. In the minimized **Page Setup** dialog box, click the **Close** button (the **X**) to return to the Sheet tab.

5. Click **Print Preview** to review the results of your selections, **Print** to print the worksheet, or **OK** to save the selections and return to the worksheet.

Set print scaling

If your worksheet content doesn't fit naturally within the space allocated to it on the page, you can scale the content for the purpose of printing, instead of modifying the content to make it fit. You can scale the worksheet manually or allow Excel to scale it for you by specifying the number of pages you want the printed worksheet to be.

To scale the worksheet when printing

➜ On the **Print** page of the Backstage view, in the **Settings** area, click **No Scaling**, and then click **Fit Sheet on One Page**, **Fit All Columns on One Page**, or **Fit All Rows on One Page**.

Or

1. On the **Print** page of the Backstage view, in the **Settings** area, click **No Scaling**, and then click **Custom Scaling Options**.

2. On the **Page** tab of the **Page Setup** dialog box, do either of the following:

   • In the **Scaling** area, click **Adjust to**, and then enter or select a scaling percentage in the **% normal size** box.

   • In the **Scaling** area, click **Fit to**. Then specify the number of pages horizontally and vertically across which you want to print the worksheet.

3. In the **Page Setup** dialog box, click **OK**.

Save workbooks in alternative file formats

You can save a workbook in multiple locations and in multiple formats.

Where once it was common only to save a file locally on your computer, many people now save files to shared locations such as Microsoft SharePoint sites, OneDrive folders, and OneDrive for Business folders for the purpose of collaborating with other people or accessing the files from multiple computers and devices.

The 2007 Microsoft Office system introduced a new set of file formats based on XML, called Microsoft Office Open XML Formats. By default, Excel 2019 workbooks are saved in the .xlsx format, which is an Excel-specific Open XML format. The .xlsx format provides the following benefits:

- File sizes are smaller than with previous file formats.
- It is simpler to recover damaged content because XML files can be opened in a variety of text editors.
- Security is greater because .xlsx files cannot contain macros, and personal data can easily be identified and removed from files.

Workbooks saved in the .xlsx format can be opened by Excel 2019, Excel 2013, Excel 2010, and Excel 2007. Users of earlier versions of Excel can download a converter that they can use to open an .xlsx file in their version of Excel.

In addition to saving a workbook for use with Excel 2019, you can save it in other formats, including the following:

- **Excel Macro-Enabled Workbook** To be able to store VBA macro code, use the XML-based .xlsm format.
- **Excel 97-2003** If you intend to share an Excel workbook specifically with users of Excel 2003 or earlier, you can save it in the .xls file format used by those versions of the program. Downgrading the file removes any unsupported formatting and features.
- **Single File Web Page or Web Page** You can convert a workbook into HTML so that it can be viewed in a web browser. Saving a workbook in the Single File Web Page format creates one .mht or .mhtml file that contains the content and supporting information, whereas saving a workbook in the Web Page format creates one .htm or .html file that sets up the display structure and a folder that contains separate content and supporting information files.

- **Excel Template** To be able to use a workbook as the starting point for other workbooks, you can save the file as a template.

- **Delimited text file** To share data from an Excel workbook with other programs, you can save it as a text file that contains tab-delimited or comma-delimited content. Saving a workbook in a text file format removes formatting and unsupported objects.

If you want people to be able to view a workbook exactly as it appears on your screen, use one of these two formats:

- **PDF (.pdf)** This format is preferred by commercial printing facilities. Recipients can display the file in the free Microsoft Reader or Adobe Reader programs and can display and edit the file in Word 2019 or Adobe Acrobat.

- **XPS (.xps)** This format precisely renders all fonts, images, and colors. Recipients can display the file in the free Microsoft Reader program or the free XPS Viewer program.

The PDF and XPS formats are designed to deliver workbooks as electronic representations of the way they appear when printed. Both types of files can easily be sent by email to many recipients and can be made available on a webpage for downloading by anyone who wants them. However, the files are no longer Excel workbooks and cannot be opened or edited in Excel.

When you save an Excel workbook in PDF or XPS format, you can optimize the file size of the document for your intended distribution method—the larger Standard file size is better for printing, whereas the Minimum file size is suitable for online publishing. You can also configure the following options:

- Specify the pages and worksheets to include in the PDF or XPS file.

- Include or exclude non-printing elements such as properties.

- Create an ISO-compliant PDF file.

IMPORTANT If you have Adobe Acrobat installed on your computer, that program might install additional tools that you can use to create PDF files from within Office programs. For example, you might have a custom Acrobat tab on the ribbon, a Save As Adobe PDF command in the left pane of the Backstage view, or a Create Adobe PDF button in the Export page of the Backstage view. When demonstrating the ability to perform tasks during the Microsoft Office Specialist exam, you can use only the built-in Excel functionality, which this book describes.

To open the Save As dialog box

→ On the **Save As** page of the Backstage view, do any of the following:

- Below the Places list, click the **Browse** button.

- Above the file navigation controls, click the file path.

- Below the file navigation controls, click the **More options** link.

→ On the **Export** page of the Backstage view, click **Change File Type**, click the file type you want, and then click **Save As**.

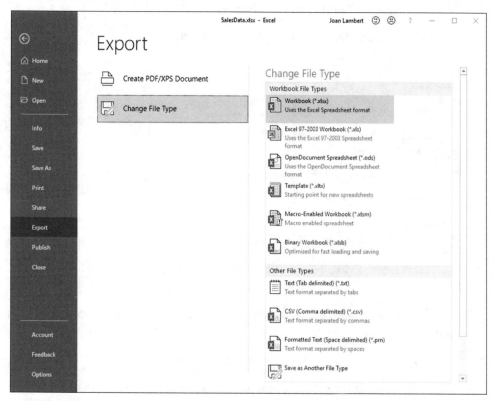

You can select a file type from the Save As dialog box or the Export page of the Backstage view

To save a file in an alternative file format with the default settings

→ On the **Save As** page of the Backstage view, browse to the folder in which you want to save the file. In the file type list at the top of the right column, click the format you want. Then click the **Save** button.

→ In the **Save As** dialog box, in the **Save as type** list, click the format you want, and then click **Save**.

→ On the **Export** page of the Backstage view, click **Change File Type**, click the file type you want, and click **Save As**. Then in the **Save As** dialog box that opens, click **Save**.

To save a file in PDF or XPS format with custom settings

1. On the **Export** page of the Backstage view, click **Create PDF/XPS Document**, and then click the **Create PDF/XPS** button.

2. In the **Publish as PDF or XPS** dialog box, click **Options**.

You can choose to include only specific worksheets or worksheet areas when saving a workbook as a PDF file

3. In the **Options** dialog box, select the options you want for the PDF or XPS file, and then click **OK**.

Or

1. Open the **Save As** dialog box. In the **Save as type** list, click either **PDF** or **XPS Document**.

2. In the **Save As** dialog box, click **Options**.

3. In the **Options** dialog box, select the options you want for the PDF or XPS file, and then click **OK**.

Exam Strategy Ensure that you are familiar with the types of file formats in which you can save Excel workbooks and when it is appropriate to use each one.

Objective 1.5 practice tasks

The practice files for these tasks are in the **MOSExcel2019\Objective1** practice file folder. The folder also contains a subfolder of result files that you can use to check your work.

➤ Open the **Excel_1-5a** workbook and do the following:

❑ Inspect the workbook for hidden properties or personal information. Review the inspection results and note the types of issues you can and can't fix from within the Document Inspector.

❑ From the Document Inspector, remove all document properties, personal information, and hidden rows from the workbook.

❑ Inspect the workbook for accessibility issues. Review the inspection results.

❑ Select one instance of each issue located and review the additional information provided by the Accessibility Checker for that issue.

❑ Fix each of the three Hard-to-read Text Contrast issues on the Data worksheet by changing the font color in the cells identified by the Accessibility Checker to Automatic (Black).

❑ Inspect the workbook for compatibility issues. Filter the results to display only issues that affect compatibility for people using Excel 2007. Go to the threaded comment identified by the Compatibility Checker and remove it.

➤ Save the **Excel_1-5a** workbook and open the **Excel_1-5a_results** workbook. Compare the two workbooks to check your work. Then close the open workbooks.

➤ Open the **Excel_1-5b** workbook and do the following:

❑ On the **Sales by Category** worksheet, set the print area so that only cells A1:B42 print.

❑ Configure the page setup options to print the worksheet gridlines, which aren't shown in the worksheet.

❑ Display the print preview of the worksheet to check your settings.

➤ Save the **Excel_1-5b** workbook and open the **Excel_1-5b_results** workbook. Compare the two workbooks to check your work. Then close the **Excel_1-5b_results** workbook.

➤ With the **Excel_1-5b** workbook open, do the following, accepting the default file locations:

❑ Save a copy of the workbook with the file name *Excel_1-5b_Compatible* in a file format that can be viewed and worked on by a colleague who is using Excel 2003. Notice the features that aren't compatible with the new file format.

❑ Save a copy of the workbook with the file name *Excel_1-5b_Template* in a file format that supports the inclusion of macros and will be available from the New page of the Backstage view so you can use it as the basis for other similar workbooks in the future.

❑ On the New page of the Backstage view, display your Personal templates and verify that the Excel_1-5b_Template file is available.

➤ Check your results against the files in the **Excel_1-5_Results** folder. Then close the open workbooks.

Objective group 2

Manage data cells and ranges

The skills tested in this section of the Microsoft Office Specialist exam for Microsoft Excel 2019 relate to managing cells and cell content in worksheets. Specifically, the following objectives are associated with this set of skills:

- **2.1** Manipulate data in worksheets
- **2.2** Format cells and ranges
- **2.3** Define and reference named ranges
- **2.4** Summarize data visually

Excel stores data in individual cells of the worksheets within a workbook. You can process or reference the data in each cell in many ways, either individually or in logical groups. A set of contiguous data cells is a *data range*. A data range can be as small as a short list of dates or as large as a multicolumn table that includes thousands of rows of data.

You might populate a worksheet from scratch or by creating, reusing, or calculating data from other sources. You can perform various operations on data when pasting it into a worksheet, either to maintain the original state of the data or to change it. When creating data from scratch, you can quickly enter large amounts of data that follows a pattern by filling a numeric or alphanumeric data series. You can fill any of the default series that come with Excel or create a custom data series.

This chapter guides you in studying ways of working with the content and appearance of cells and the organization of data.

IMPORTANT If you apply an Excel table format to a data range, it then becomes a table, which has additional functionality beyond that of a data range. Tables are discussed in Objective group 3, "Manage tables and table data." The functionality in this chapter pertains explicitly to data ranges that are not formatted as Excel tables.

Objective 2.1: Manipulate data in worksheets

The most basic method of inserting data in cells is by entering it manually, which is a prerequisite skill for this exam. This section discusses methods of creating and reusing data to fill a worksheet.

Create data

When you create the structure of a data range, or a series of formulas, you can automate the process of completing data patterns (such as *January*, *February*, *March*) or copying calculations from one row or column to those adjacent. Automation saves time and can help prevent human errors.

You can quickly fill adjacent cells with data that continues a formula or a series of numbers, days, or dates, either manually from the Fill menu, or automatically by dragging the fill handle. When copying or filling data by using the Fill menu commands, you can set specific options in the Series dialog box for the pattern of the data sequence you want to create.

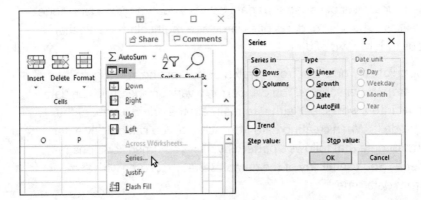

The Fill menu and Series dialog box

You can use the fill functionality to copy text data, numeric data, or cell formatting (such as text color, background color, and alignment) to adjacent cells.

When creating a series based on one or more selected cells (called *filling a series*), you can select from the following series types:

- **Linear** Excel calculates the series values by adding the value you enter in the Step Value box to each cell in the series.

- **Growth** Excel calculates the series values by multiplying each cell in the series by the step value.

- **Date** Excel calculates the series values by incrementing each cell in the series of dates, designated by the Date Unit you select, by the step value.

- **Auto Fill** This option creates a series that produces the same results as dragging the fill handle.

When you use the Auto Fill feature, either from the Fill menu or by dragging the fill handle, the Auto Fill Options button appears in the lower-right corner of the fill range. Clicking the button displays a menu of fill options. The fill options vary based on the type of content being filled.

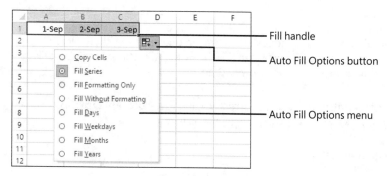

The Auto Fill Options menu when filling a date series

Tip The Auto Fill Options button does not appear when you copy data to adjacent cells.

You can use the Auto Fill feature to create sequences of numbers, days, and dates; to apply formatting from one cell to adjacent cells; or, if you use Excel for more sophisticated purposes, to create sequences of data generated by formulas, or custom sequences based on information you specify. You can also use the fill functionality to copy text or numeric data within the column or row.

To fill a simple numeric, day, or date series

1. Do either of the following:

   - In the upper-left cell of the range you want to fill, enter the first number, day, or date of the series you want to create.

   - To create a series in which numbers or dates increment by more than one, enter the first two or more values of the series in the first cells of the range you want to fill.

   Tip Enter as many numbers or dates as are necessary to establish the series.

   ---

2. If creating a numeric series that has a specific number format (such as currency, percentage, or fraction), apply the number format you want from the **Number** group on the **Home** tab.

3. Select the cell or cells that define the series.

4. Do either of the following:

   - Drag the fill handle down or to the right to create an increasing series.

   - Drag the fill handle up or to the left to create a decreasing series.

   Tip When using the fill handle, you can drag in only one direction at a time; to fill a range of multiple columns and rows, first drag in one direction, then release the mouse button and drag the new fill handle in the other direction. The default fill series value is indicated in a tooltip as you drag.

   ---

5. If the series doesn't automatically fill correctly, click the **Auto Fill Options** button and then, on the **Auto Fill Options** menu, click **Fill Series**.

To fill a specific day or date series

1. Fill the series. Immediately after you release the mouse button, click the **Auto Fill Options** button that appears in the lower-right corner of the cell range.

2. On the **Auto Fill Options** menu, click **Fill Days**, **Fill Weekdays**, **Fill Months**, or **Fill Years**.

To set advanced options for a numeric, day, or date series

1. Enter the number or date beginning the series, and then select the cell range you want to fill.

2. On the **Home** tab, in the **Editing** group, in the **Fill** list, click **Series**.

3. In the **Series** dialog box, select the options you want, and then click **OK**.

To exclude formatting when filling or copying data

1. Drag the fill handle to fill the series or copy the data, and then click the **Auto Fill Options** button.

2. On the **Auto Fill Options** menu, click **Fill Without Formatting**.

Reuse data

If the content you want to work with in Excel already exists elsewhere—such as in another worksheet or workbook or in a document—you can cut or copy the data from the source location to the Microsoft Office Clipboard and then paste it into the worksheet. If the content exists but not in the format that you need it, you might be able to reform the content to fit your needs by using the CONCATENATE function or the Flash Fill feature.

Paste data by using special paste options

You can insert cut or copied cell contents into empty cells or directly into an existing table or data range. Cutting, copying, and pasting content (including columns and rows) in a worksheet are basic tasks that, as a certification candidate, you should have extensive experience with. If you need a refresher on these subjects, see the "Prerequisites" section of the Exam Overview. This section contains information about Excel-specific pasting operations that you may be required to demonstrate to pass Exam MO-200 and become certified as a Microsoft Office Specialist for Excel 2019.

When pasting data, you have several options for inserting values, formulas, formatting, or links to the original source data into the new location. Paste options are available from the Paste menu, from the shortcut menu, and from the Paste Options menu that becomes temporarily available when you paste content.

Excel also offers some advanced pasting techniques you can use to modify data while pasting it into a worksheet. Using the Paste Special feature, you can perform mathematical operations when you paste data over existing data, you can transpose columns to rows and rows to columns, and you can be selective about what you want to paste from the source cells.

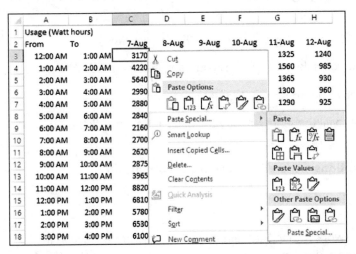

The available paste options vary based on the type and formatting of the content you're pasting

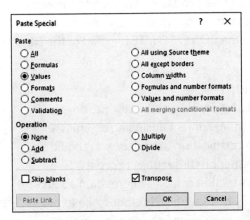

Paste specific aspects of copied content, or modify content while pasting it

You have the option to paste only values without formatting, formatting without values, formulas, comments, and other specific aspects of copied content. You can also link to data rather than inserting it, so that if the source data changes, the copied data will also change.

Paste options that are commonly used in business, and that you should be comfortable with when taking Exam MO-200, include the following:

- **Pasting values** When you reuse a value that is the result of a formula, it is often necessary to paste only the value—the result of the formula—rather than the actual cell content.

- **Pasting formats** This is somewhat like using the Format Painter and can be useful when you want to build a structure on a worksheet that already exists elsewhere.

- **Transposing cells** Transposing content switches it from columns to rows or from rows to columns. This can be very useful when reusing content from one worksheet in another.

Original data   Transposed data

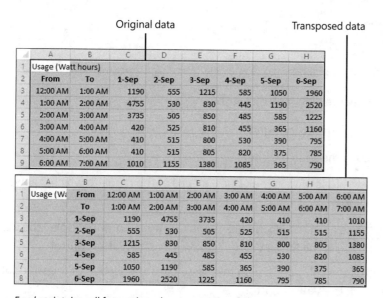

Excel maintains cell formatting when transposing data

Exam Strategy Be familiar with all the Paste and Paste Special options.

To insert data into an existing data range

1. Select and copy the source content.

2. Select the upper-left cell of the range in which you want to insert the copied content.

3. On the **Home** tab, in the **Cells** group, click **Insert**, and then click **Insert Copied Cells**.

4. In the **Insert Paste** dialog box, click **Shift cells right** or **Shift cells down** to indicate the direction you want Excel to move the existing content.

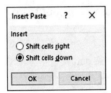

Specify the direction to shift existing data when inserting cells into a data range

5. In the **Insert Paste** dialog box, click **OK**.

To paste cell values (without formulas)

1. Select and copy the source content.

2. Do either of the following in the upper-left cell of the range to which you want to copy the values:

    *   Select the cell. On the **Home** tab, in the **Clipboard** group, display the **Paste** list and then, in the **Paste Values** section, click the **Values** button.

    *   Right-click the cell, and then in the **Paste Options** section of the shortcut menu, click the **Values** button.

To paste cell formatting (without content)

1. Select and copy the formatted source content.

2. Do either of the following in the upper-left cell of the range to which you want to copy the values:

    *   Select the cell. On the **Home** tab, in the **Clipboard** group, display the **Paste** list and then, in the **Other Paste Options** section, click the **Formatting** button.

    *   Right-click the cell, and then in the **Paste Options** section of the shortcut menu, click the **Formatting** button.

To transpose rows and columns

1. Select and copy the source content.

2. Do either of the following in the upper-left cell of the range to which you want to copy the transposed values:

   - Select the cell. On the **Home** tab, in the **Clipboard** group, display the **Paste** list and then, in the **Paste** section, click the **Transpose** button.

   - Right-click the cell, and then in the **Paste Options** section of the shortcut menu, click the **Transpose** button.

Tip Transposing data retains its formatting.

Fill data based on an adjacent column

The Flash Fill feature looks for correlation between data that you enter in a column and the adjacent data. If it identifies a pattern of data entry based on the adjacent column, it fills the rest of the column to match the pattern. A common example of using Flash Fill is to divide full names in one column into separate columns of first and last names so you can reference them individually (for example, when creating form letters).

	A	B	C	D
1	Exam Objective	Number	Description	
2	2. Manage Data Cells and Ranges	2	Manage Data Cells and Ranges	
3	2.1 Manipulate data in worksheets	2.1	Manipulate data in worksheets	
4	2.1.1 Paste data by using special paste options	2.1.1	Paste data by using special paste options	
5	2.1.2 Fill cells by using Auto Fill	2.1.2	Fill cells by using Auto Fill	
6	2.1.3 Insert and delete multiple columns or rows	2.1.3	Insert and delete multiple c...	Undo Flash Fill
7	2.1.4 Insert and delete cells	2.1.4	Insert and delete cells	Accept suggestions
8	2.2 Format cells and ranges	2.2	Format cells and ranges	Select all 0 blank cells
9	2.2.1 Merge and unmerge cells	2.2.1	Merge and unmerge cells	Select all 20 changed cells
10	2.2.2 Modify cell alignment, orientation, and indentation	2.2.2	Modify cell alignment, orien...	
11	2.2.3 Format cells by using Format Painter	2.2.3	Format cells by using Format Painter	
12	2.2.4 Wrap text within cells	2.2.4	Wrap text within cells	
13	2.2.5 Apply number formats	2.2.5	Apply number formats	
14	2.2.6 Apply cell formats from the Format Cells dialog box	2.2.6	Apply cell formats from the Format Cells dialog box	
15	2.2.7 Apply cell styles	2.2.7	Apply cell styles	
16	2.2.8 Clear cell formatting	2.2.8	Clear cell formatting	
17	2.3 Define and reference named ranges	2.3	Define and reference named ranges	
18	2.3.1 Define a named range	2.3.1	Define a named range	
19	2.3.2 Name a table	2.3.2	Name a table	
20	2.4 Summarize data visually	2.4	Summarize data visually	
21	2.4.1 Insert Sparklines	2.4.1	Insert Sparklines	
22	2.4.2 Apply built-in conditional formatting	2.4.2	Apply built-in conditional formatting	
23	2.4.3 Remove conditional formatting	2.4.3	Remove conditional formatting	

Flash Fill automatically fills cells with content from adjacent columns

To fill cells by using Flash Fill

1. In columns adjacent to the source content column, enter content in one or more cells to establish the pattern of content reuse.

2. Select the next cell below the cells that establish the pattern. (Do not select a range of cells.)

3. Do either of the following:

   - On the **Home** tab, in the **Editing** group, click **Fill**, and then click **Flash Fill**.

   - Press **Ctrl+E**.

Tip If the Flash Fill operation doesn't work as intended, click the Flash Fill Options button that appears in the lower-right corner of the first filled cell and then, on the menu, click Undo Flash Fill. Enter content in additional cells to further establish the pattern, and then try again.

Modify worksheet structure

Insert and delete multiple columns or rows

To insert rows or columns

1. Select the number of rows you want to insert, starting with the row above which you want the inserted rows to appear, or select the number of columns you want to insert, starting with the column to the left of which you want the inserted columns to appear.

2. Do either of the following:

   - On the **Home** tab, in the **Cells** group, click the **Insert** button.

   - Right-click the selection, and then click **Insert**.

To delete selected rows or columns

→ On the **Home** tab, in the **Cells** group, click the **Delete** button.

→ Right-click the selection, and then click **Delete**.

Insert and delete cells

To insert cells in an existing data range

1. Select the number of cells you want to insert, in the location in which you want to insert them.

2. On the **Home** tab, in the **Cells** group, click **Insert** and then **Insert Cells**.

3. In the **Insert** dialog box, select **Shift cells right** or **Shift cells down** to indicate the direction in which you want to move the existing data to make room for the new cells. Then click **OK**.

2

Objective 2.1 practice tasks

The practice file for these tasks is in the **MOSExcel2019\Objective2** practice file folder. The folder also contains a result file that you can use to check your work.

➤ Open the **Excel_2-1** workbook, and complete the following tasks by using the data in cells B4:G9 of the **Ad Buy Constraints** worksheet:

❑ Paste only the values and formatting into the range beginning at B18.

❑ Paste only the formulas into the range beginning at B25.

❑ Paste only the formatting (but not the content) into the range beginning at B32.

❑ Delete rows to move the headings to row 1.

❑ Delete columns to move the Magazine column to column A.

❑ Cut the data from the Mag3 row (B4:F4) and insert it into the Mag2 row (B3:F3).

❑ Move the *Cost Per Ad* data to the left of the Total Cost cells.

❑ Insert two blank cells in positions B8:B9, shifting any existing data down.

❑ Transpose the names in the Magazine column (cells A1:A6) to the first row of a new worksheet.

➤ On the **Price List** worksheet, do the following:

❑ Using the fill handle, fill cells A2:A21 with *Item 1*, *Item 2*, *Item 3*, and so on through *Item 20*.

❑ Fill cells B2:B21 with *10*, *20*, *30*, and so on through *200*.

❑ Fill cells C2:C21 with *$3.00*, *$2.95*, *$2.90*, and so on through *$2.05*.

❑ Copy the background and font formatting from cell A1 to cells A2:A21. Then delete the content of cell A1 (but not the cell).

➤ Save the **Excel_2-1** workbook and open the **Excel_2-1_results** workbook. Compare the two workbooks to check your work. Then close the open workbooks.

Objective 2.2: Format cells and ranges

Merge and unmerge cells

Worksheets that involve data at multiple hierarchical levels often use horizontal and vertical merged cells to clearly delineate relationships. Excel provides the following three merge options:

- **Merge & Center** This option merges the cells across the selected rows and columns and centers the data from the first selected cell in the merged cell.

- **Merge Across** This option creates a separate merged cell for each row in the selection area and maintains default alignment for the data type of the first cell of each row of the merged cells.

- **Merge Cells** This option merges the cells across the selected rows and columns and maintains default alignment for the data type of the first cell of the merged cells.

In the case of Merge & Center and Merge Cells, data in selected cells other than the first is deleted. In the case of Merge Across, data in selected cells other than the first cell of each row is deleted.

Merged columns

Merged rows

	Monday		Tuesday		Wednesday		Thursday		Friday		
	15-Jul		16-Jul		17-Jul		18-Jul		19-Jul		
Time In		Total		Total		Total		Total		Total	Weekly
Time Out		0.0		0.0		0.0		0.0		0.0	Total
	Meal Break										
Time In		Total		Total		Total		Total		Total	
Time Out		0.0		0.0		0.0		0.0		0.0	
Total	0.0		0.0		0.0		0.0		0.0		0.0

Merging columns or rows retains the content of the first cell

To merge selected cells

→ On the **Home** tab, in the **Alignment** group, click the **Merge & Center** button to center and bottom-align the entry from the first cell.

→ On the **Home** tab, in the **Alignment** group, display the **Merge & Center** list, and then click **Merge Across** to create a separate merged cell on each selected row, maintaining the horizontal alignment of the data type in the first cell of each row.

→ On the **Home** tab, in the **Alignment** group, display the **Merge & Center** list, and then click **Merge Cells** to merge the entire selection, maintaining the horizontal alignment of the data type in the first cell.

To unmerge selected cells

→ On the **Home** tab, in the **Alignment** group, click the **Merge & Center** button to deselect it.

Modify cell alignment, orientation, and indentation

Structural formatting can be applied to a cell, a row, a column, or the entire worksheet. However, some kinds of formatting can detract from the readability of a worksheet if they are applied haphazardly.

Budget drivers	Scenario 1 (Best case)	Scenario 2 (Average case)	Scenario 3 (Worst case)
Probability of shipping on time	98%	95%	90%
Building permits issued in prior quarter	10000	12500	15000
Regional economic growth	4%	3%	2%
Competitive strength (products, pricing, promotion, placement)	7	8	9
Probability of key supplier performance	99%	95%	90%

Structural cell formatting

Tip By default, row height is dynamic and increases to fit the text in its cells. If you manually change the height of a row and then change the size or amount of content in that row, you might have to set or reset the row height. For information about adjusting row height, see "Objective 1.3: Format worksheets and workbooks."

The formatting you might typically apply to a row or column includes the following:

- **Alignment** You can specify a horizontal alignment (Left, Center, Right, Fill, Justify, Center Across Selection, and Distributed) and vertical alignment (Top, Center, Bottom, Justify, or Distributed) of a cell's contents. The defaults are Left and Top, but in many cases another alignment will be more appropriate.

- **Orientation** By default, entries are horizontal and read from left to right. You can rotate entries for special effect or to allow you to display more information on the screen or a printed page. This capability is particularly useful when you have long column headings above columns of short entries.

- **Indentation** You can specify an indent distance from the left or right side when you choose those horizontal alignments, or from both sides when you choose a distributed horizontal alignment. A common reason for indenting cells is to create a list of subitems without using a second column.

Tip You can change the text alignment, text control, text direction, and text orientation settings on the Alignment tab of the Format Cells dialog box. There are many ways to open the Format Cells dialog box to a specific tab. You may use any method you want.

To open the Format Cells dialog box to the most recently used tab

→ On the **Home** tab, click the **Font** dialog box launcher.

→ Press **Ctrl+1**.

To align entries within selected cells

→ On the **Home** tab, in the **Alignment** group, click the **Align Left**, **Center**, or **Align Right** button to specify horizontal alignment, or click the **Top Align**, **Middle Align**, or **Bottom Align** button to specify vertical alignment.

→ On the **Home** tab, click the **Alignment** dialog box launcher. On the **Alignment** tab of the **Format Cells** dialog box, in the **Horizontal** and **Vertical** lists, click the cell alignment you want.

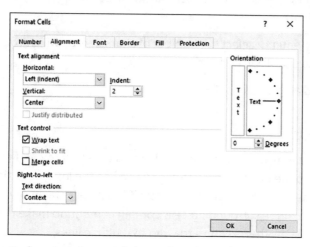

Configure text alignment, indents, orientation, and wrapping options at one time from the Format Cells dialog box

✧✧

Exam Strategy Many more text alignment options are available from the Format Cells dialog box than from the Format group of the Home tab. Ensure that you are familiar with these options.

✧✧

To change the orientation of the text in selected cells

1. On the **Home** tab, in the **Alignment** group, click the **Orientation** button to display the Alignment tab of the Format Cells dialog box.

2. In the **Orientation** area, do either of the following:

   - Drag the red diamond to the angle you want.

   - In the **Degrees** list, click the angle you want.

   The *Text* preview changes to display the effect of your selection.

3. In the **Format Cells** dialog box, click **OK**.

To indent the content of selected cells

1. On the **Home** tab, click the **Alignment** dialog box launcher.

2. On the **Alignment** tab of the **Format Cells** dialog box, in the **Text alignment** section, do the following:

   a. In the **Horizontal** list, select **Left (Indent)**, **Right (Indent)**, or **Distributed (Indent)**.

   b. In the **Indent** box, enter or select the number of characters by which you want to indent the text. Then click **OK**.

3. In the **Format Cells** dialog box, click **OK**.

Wrap text within cells

By default, Excel does not wrap text in a cell. Instead, it allows the entry to overflow into the surrounding cells (to the right from a left-aligned cell, to the left from a right-aligned cell, and to both sides from a center-aligned cell) if those cells are empty, or it hides the part that won't fit if the surrounding cells contain content. To make the entire entry visible, you can allow the cell entry to wrap to multiple lines.

Tip Wrapping text increases the height of the cell. Increasing the height of one cell increases the height of the entire row.

To wrap long entries in selected cells

→ On the **Home** tab, in the **Alignment** group, click the **Wrap Text** button.

Apply cell formats and styles

By default, the font used for text in a new Excel worksheet is 11-point Calibri, but you can use the same techniques you would use in any Office 2019 program to change the font and the following font attributes:

- Size
- Style
- Color
- Underline

As a certification candidate, you should be very familiar with methods of applying character formatting from the Font group on the Home tab, from the Mini Toolbar, and from the Font, Border, and Fill tabs of the Format Cells dialog box.

Cell Styles are preconfigured sets of cell formats, some tied to the workbook theme colors and some with implied meanings. You can standardize formatting throughout workbooks by applying cell styles to content.

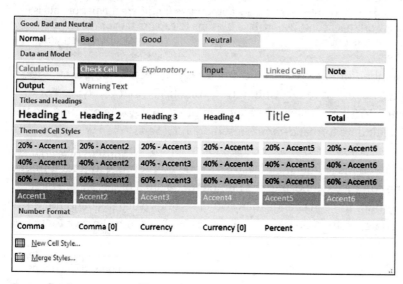

Some cell styles connote specific meanings

⋄⋄⋄

Exam Strategy Exam MO-200 requires that you demonstrate the ability to apply built-in cell styles. Creating custom cell styles is part of the objective domain for Exam MO-201, Microsoft Excel Expert.

⋄⋄⋄

To apply cell formatting from the Format Cells dialog box to selected cells

1.   On the **Home** tab, click the **Font** dialog box launcher.

2.   In the **Format Cells** dialog box, on the **Font**, **Border**, and **Fill** tabs, select the formatting you want to apply to the cell and its content. Then click **OK**.

To apply a cell style to a selected cell

1.   On the **Home** tab, in the **Styles** group, click the **Cell Styles** button.

2.   In the **Cell Styles** gallery, click the style you want.

Apply number formats

By default, all the cells in a new worksheet are assigned the General number format. When setting up or populating a worksheet, you assign to cells the number format that is most appropriate for the type of information they contain. The format determines not only how the information looks, but also how Excel can work with it.

⋄⋄⋄

Exam Strategy Knowing which number formats are appropriate for different types of data is important for efficient worksheet construction. Take the time to explore the formats so that you understand the available options.

⋄⋄⋄

You can assign a number format to a cell before or after you enter a number in it. You can also just start typing and have Excel intuit the format from what you type. (For example, if you enter *9/15*, Excel makes the educated guess that you're entering a date and applies the default date format *d-mmm*, resulting in *15-Sep*.) When you allow Excel to assign a number format, or you choose a format from the Number Format list in the Number group on the Home tab, Excel uses the default settings for that format. You can change the currency symbol and the number of decimal places shown directly from the Number group. You can change many other settings (such as changing the format of calendar dates from *15-Sep* to *September 15, 2019*) from the Format Cells dialog box.

Exam Strategy Exam MO-200 requires you to demonstrate that you can apply built-in number formats. Creating custom number formats is part of the objective domain for Exam MO-201, Microsoft Excel Expert.

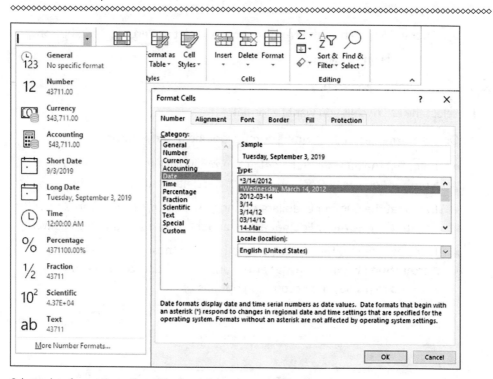

Select a data format that will provide clear information to workbook readers

When you apply the Percentage number format to a cell, the cell displays the percentage equivalent of the number. For example, the number 1 is shown as 100%, the number 5 as 500%, or the number 0.25 as 25%.

Tip On the Home tab, in the Number group, the button that applies the Percentage style has the ScreenTip *Percent Style*.

To apply a default number format to selected cells

➜ On the **Home** tab, in the **Number** group, display the **Number Format** list, and then click a format.

Tip If you want a number to be treated as text, apply the Text number format.

To display the percentage equivalent of a number

1. Select the cell or cells you want to format.

2. Do either of the following:

    *   On the **Home** tab, in the **Number** group, click the **Percent Style** button.

    *   Press **Ctrl+Shift+%**.

To display a number as currency

1. Select the cell or cells you want to format.

2. On the **Home** tab, in the **Number** group, do one of the following:

    *   To format the number in the default currency, click the **Accounting Number Format** button (labeled with the default currency symbol).

    *   To format the number in dollars, pounds, euros, yen, or Swiss francs, click the **Accounting Number Format** arrow, and then click the currency you want.

    *   To format the number in a currency other than those listed, click the **Accounting Number Format** arrow, and then click **More Accounting Formats** to display the Accounting options.

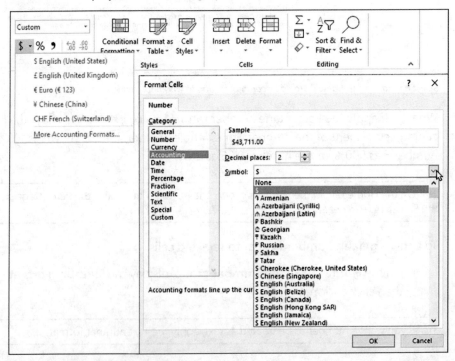

You can choose from hundreds of currencies

3. In the **Format Cells** dialog box, do the following, and then click **OK**:

   a. In the **Symbol** list, select the currency symbol you want to display.

   b. In the **Decimal places** box, enter or select the number of decimal places you want to display.

To display more or fewer decimal places for numbers

1. Select the cell or cells you want to format.

2. On the **Home** tab, in the **Number** group, do either of the following:

   - To display more decimal places, click the **Increase Decimal** button.

   - To display fewer (or no) decimal places, click the **Decrease Decimal** button.

To apply a number format with settings other than the default

1. Select the cell or cells you want to format.

2. On the **Home** tab, click the **Number** dialog box launcher.

3. On the **Number** tab of the **Format Cells** dialog box, select the type of number in the **Category** list.

4. Configure the settings that are specific to the number category, and then click **OK**.

Exam Strategy Exam MO-200 requires that you demonstrate the ability to apply built-in number formats. Creating and managing custom number formats is part of the objective domain for Exam MO-201, Microsoft Excel Expert.

Reapply existing formatting

If you apply a series of formats to one or more cells—for example, if you format cell content as 14-point, bold, centered, red text—and then want to apply the same combination of formatting to other cells, you can copy the formatting. You can use the fill functionality to copy formatting to adjacent content, or use the Format Painter to copy formatting anywhere. When using the Format Painter, you first copy existing formatting from one or more cells, and then paste the formatting to other cells. You can use the Format Painter to paste copied formatting only once or to remain active until you turn it off.

To copy existing formatting to other cells

1. Select the cell that has the formatting you want to copy.

2. On the **Mini Toolbar** or in the **Clipboard** group on the **Home** tab, click the **Format Painter** button once if you want to apply the copied formatting only once, or twice if you want to apply the copied formatting multiple times.

3. With the paintbrush-shaped cursor, click or select the cell or cells to which you want to apply the copied formatting.

4. If you clicked the **Format Painter** button twice, click or select additional cells you want to format. Then click the **Format Painter** button again, or press the **Esc** key, to turn off the Format Painter.

To fill formatting to adjacent cells

1. Select the cell that has the formatting you want to copy.

2. Drag the fill handle up, down, to the left, or to the right to encompass the cells you want to format.

3. On the **Auto Fill Options** menu, click **Fill Formatting Only**.

Objective 2.2 practice tasks

The practice file for these tasks is in the **MOSExcel2019\Objective2** practice file folder. The folder also contains a result file that you can use to check your work.

➤ Open the **Excel_2-2** workbook, display the **Employees** worksheet, and do the following:

❑ Merge cells A13:C14 so that the hyperlink is centered in a double-height cell across the three columns.

➤ On the **Expense Statement** worksheet, do the following:

❑ Select the entire worksheet and turn on text wrapping.

❑ Turn off text wrapping in only rows 4, 5, and 9.

❑ Right-align the entries in column A.

❑ Bottom-align the headings in row 9.

❑ Apply the *Angle Counterclockwise* orientation to the headings in row 9.

❑ Format cell K10 to display its contents as currency with a US dollar symbol and no decimal places. Then apply the same formatting to cells K11:K23.

❑ Apply the *20% - Accent2* cell style to cells A9:K9.

➤ Save the **Excel_2-2** workbook and open the **Excel_2-2_results** workbook. Compare the two workbooks to check your work. Then close the open workbooks.

Objective 2.3: Define and reference named ranges

As specified at the beginning of this chapter, a set of contiguous data cells is a *data range*. Data ranges are expressed in the format *upper-left cell:lower-right cell*—for example, A1:J10 defines the 100 cells within the area bound by cells A1 in the upper-left corner, J1 in the upper-right corner, J10 in the lower-right corner, and A10 in the lower-left corner. You can reference a data range (A1:J10) in a formula, or you can give the range a meaningful name (such as *StudentGrades* or *PriceList*) and then reference the range name. Using named ranges can greatly simplify formulaic processes because you don't have to find or remember the cell references, and if you add data to a named range, the new data is automatically included in any formulas that reference the range.

Excel tables are assigned names automatically when you create them. Within each workbook, the first table you create is Table1, then Table2, and so on. You can reference any table by its default name or change the numeric table names to something more meaningful so you can more easily reference them.

The Name Manager, which is available from the Formula tab of the Ribbon, displays all named objects in the active workbook.

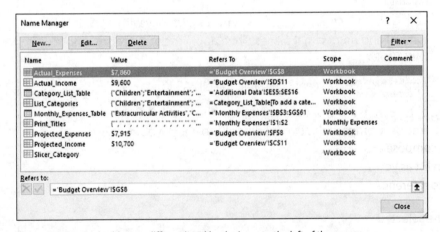

Named ranges and tables are differentiated by the icons to the left of the names

Exam Strategy Each named object has a scope within which it can be referenced—either a specific worksheet or the entire workbook. Modifying the scope of a named object is beyond the scope of exam MO-200, Microsoft Excel Associate.

You can create and modify range names and table names (or the data defined by those names) from the Name Manager. However, if you're simply naming a range or renaming a table, there's an easier way:

- You can name data ranges from the Name box at the left end of the Formula Bar.

- You can rename tables from the Table Name box in the Properties group of the Design tool tab for tables.

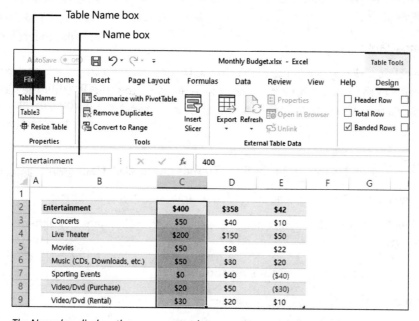

The Name box displays the range name when an entire named range is selected

When you compose a formula from the Formula Bar, named objects appear in a drop-down list as you enter the first characters of the name. You can select the object you want to reference from the list to avoid spelling errors.

To name the selected cell range

➜ In the **Name** box at the left end of the **Formula Bar**, replace the cell reference with the name, and then press **Enter**.

To simultaneously name the selected cell range and define its scope

1. Do one of the following:

   - Right-click the selection, and then click **Define Name**.
   - On the **Formulas** tab, in the **Defined Names** group, click **Define Name**.
   - On the **Formulas** tab, in the **Defined Names** group, click **Name Manager**, and then in the **Name Manager** dialog box, click **New...** .

2. In the **New Name** dialog box, enter the range name, select the scope, and then click **OK**.

To rename a table

→ Select or click any cell in the table. On the **Design** tool tab, in the **Properties** group, in the **Table Name** box, click the table name to select it, enter the name you want to assign to the table, and then press **Enter**.

Or

1. On the **Formulas** tab, in the **Defined Names** group, click **Name Manager**.

2. In the **Name Manager** window, click the table, and then click **Edit**.

3. In the **Edit Name** dialog box, select and replace the table name, and then click **OK**.

To reference a named range or table in a formula

1. In the formula, begin typing the range name or table name.

2. In the list that appears, select the named object you want to reference in the formula.

Objective 2.3 practice tasks

The practice file for these tasks is in the **MOSExcel2019\Objective2** practice file folder. The folder also contains a result file that you can use to check your work.

➤ Open the **Excel_2-3** workbook, display the **Monthly** worksheet, and do the following:

❑ Rename *Table1* as **MonthlySales**.

➤ Display the **Quarterly** worksheet, and do the following:

❑ Select cells B2:E5 and name the range **QuarterlySales**.

❑ In cell H2, use the MAX() function and the range name to display the maximum value of the *QuarterlySales* range.

➤ Save the **Excel_2-3** workbook. Open the **Excel_2-3_results** workbook. Compare the two workbooks to check your work. Then close the open workbooks.

Objective 2.4: Summarize data visually

Format cells based on their content

You can make worksheet data easier to interpret by using conditional formatting to format cells based on their values. If a value meets a specific condition, Excel applies the formatting; if it doesn't, the formatting is not applied.

	A	B	C	D	E	F	G	H	I	J
1	Usage (Watt hours)									
2	From	To	1-Sep	2-Sep	3-Sep	4-Sep	5-Sep	6-Sep	7-Sep	8-Sep
3	12:00 AM	1:00 AM	1190	555	1215	585	1050	1960	1050	675
4	1:00 AM	2:00 AM	4755	530	830	445	1190	2520	610	625
5	2:00 AM	3:00 AM	3735	505	850	485	585	1225	525	590
6	3:00 AM	4:00 AM	420	525	810	455	365	1160	450	555
7	4:00 AM	5:00 AM	410	515	800	530	390	795	450	670
8	5:00 AM	6:00 AM	410	515	805	820	375	785	440	545
9	6:00 AM	7:00 AM	1010	1155	1380	1085	365	790	435	565
10	7:00 AM	8:00 AM	1940	1980	2065	615	445	870	675	510
11	8:00 AM	9:00 AM	1870	1900	2090	455	435	925	770	755
12	9:00 AM	10:00 AM	1920	1955	2770	1605	1630	2765	1790	2085
13	10:00 AM	11:00 AM	1895	1845	2840	1710	2055	2105	1745	1980
14	11:00 AM	12:00 PM	1835	1755	5230	1915	3160	2115	1815	2500

Color scales and other conditional formatting can make it easy to quickly identify data trends

You set up conditional formatting by specifying the condition, which is called a *formatting rule*. You can select from the following types of rules:

- **Highlight cells** Apply formatting to cells that contain data within a specified numeric range, contain specific text, or contain duplicate values.

- **Top/bottom** Apply formatting to cells that contain the highest or lowest values in a range.

- **Data bars** Fill a portion of each cell corresponding to the relationship of the cell's data to the rest of the data in the selected range.

- **Color scales** Fill each cell with a color point from a two-color or three-color gradient that corresponds to the relationship of the cell's data to the rest of the data in the selected range.

- **Icon sets** Insert an icon from a selected set that corresponds to the relationship of the cell's data to the rest of the data in the selected range.

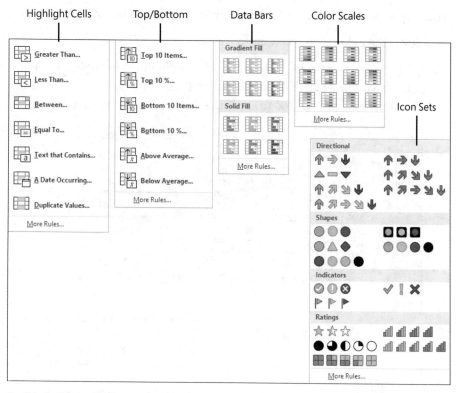

Excel includes many built-in conditional formatting options

◇◇

Exam Strategy Familiarize yourself with the types of conditional formatting rules and their variations so that you know how to quickly apply any condition that might be requested on the exam.

Exam MO-200 requires that you demonstrate the ability to apply built-in conditional formatting rules to static data. Creating custom conditional formatting rules and applying rules based on formula results are part of the objective domain for Exam MO-201, Microsoft Excel Expert.

◇◇

To quickly apply the default value of a conditional formatting rule

1. Select the data range you want to format.

2. Click the **Quick Analysis** button that appears in the lower-right corner of the selection (or press **Ctrl+Q**) and then click **Data Bars**, **Color Scale**, **Icon Set**, **Greater Than**, or **Top 10%** to apply the default rule and formatting.

1-Sep	2-Sep	3-Sep	4-Sep	5-Sep	6-Sep	7-Sep	8-Sep	9-Sep
1190	555	1215	585	1050	1960	1050	675	760
4755	530	830	445	1190	2520	610	625	550
3735	505	850	485	585	1225	525	590	525
420	525	810	455	365	1160	450	555	550
410	515	800	530	390	795	450	670	540
410	515	805	820	375	785	440	545	530
1010	1155	1380	1085	365	790	435	565	535
1940	1980	2065	615	445	870	675	510	750
1870	1900	2090	455	435	925	770	755	760
1920	1955	2770	1605	1630	2765	1790	2085	2065
1895	1845	2840	1710	2055	2105	1745	1980	2305
1835	1755	5230	1915	3160	2115	1815	2500	2135

Formatting   Charts   Totals   Tables   Sparklines

Data Bars   Color...   Icon Set   Greater...   Top 10%   Clear...

Conditional Formatting uses rules to highlight interesting data.

The Quick Analysis menu provides easy access to default conditional formatting

To format font color and cell fill in the selected data range based on a specified condition

1. On the **Home** tab, in the **Styles** group, click the **Conditional Formatting** button.

2. In the **Conditional Formatting** list, point to **Highlight Cell Rules** or **Top/Bottom Rules**, and then click the type of condition you want to specify.

3. In the dialog box, specify the parameters of the condition, click the formatting combination you want, and then click **OK**.

To apply formatting based on the relationship of values in the selected data range

→ In the **Conditional Formatting** list, point to **Data Bars**, **Color Scales**, or **Icon Sets**, and then click the formatting option you want.

To remove conditional formatting from selected cells

→ In the **Conditional Formatting** list, point to **Clear Rules**, and then click **Clear Rules from Selected Cells** or **Clear Rules from Entire Sheet**.

→ Open the **Conditional Formatting Rules Manager** dialog box, click the rule, click **Delete Rule**, and then click **OK**.

Insert sparklines

Excel worksheets can store vast quantities of numeric data. Because this data can be difficult to interpret, many Excel users choose to represent the data in a chart to give it a meaningful form. If you want to provide a visual key alongside the data, you can display sparklines to provide the user with information about how each entry within a data range relates to those around it.

Sparklines are miniature charts that summarize worksheet data in a single cell. Excel 2019 includes three types of sparklines: Line, Column, and Win/Loss. Line and Column sparklines resemble charts of the same types. A Win/Loss sparkline indicates whether each data point is positive, zero, or negative.

	L	M	N	O	P	Q	R	S	T	U
1										
2	10-Sep	11-Sep	12-Sep	13-Sep	14-Sep	15-Sep	16-Sep	17-Sep	18-Sep	
3										
4	1870	995	960	835	1245	395	1190	900	820	
5	575	945	1150	855	575	405	430	2475	465	
6	540	1000	1020	785	385	400	430	1035	425	
7	555	895	505	835	350	395	425	460	430	
8	540	900	485	765	385	550	430	440	455	
9	560	880	495	800	395	470	430	450	420	
10	545	860	460	785	380	395	425	400	405	
11	615	1125	645	875	550	2655	635	455	475	
12	615	930	690	3070	495	3670	1780	470	475	
13	1790	2025	1890	3770	1645	3865	2360	1575	1600	
14	1825	2045	1930	3150	1830	3735	2200	2195	1705	
15	1810	4645	1770	3155	1975	1900	3680	2100	1700	
16	2140	4730	1760	3100	1760	3125	2660	2955	1825	
17	1960	1965	1730	2695	1760	3650	2085	3800	1755	

Line sparklines (at the top) and column sparklines (on the side) help identify data patterns

A sparkline consists of a series of markers. Depending on the sparkline type, you can choose to accentuate the first or last point in the data series, the high or low value, or the negative values, by displaying a marker of a different color.

You can apply styles and other formatting to sparklines in the same way that you do to other graphic elements, by using commands on the Design tool tab that appears when a sparkline is selected.

Emphasize specific markers

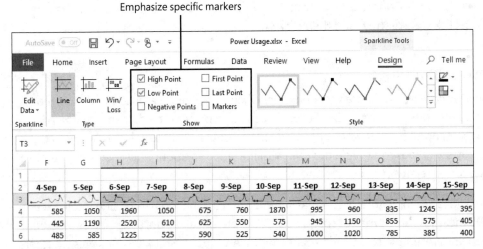

Sparkline colors are linked to the workbook theme

To create a sparkline or sparklines

1. Select the data you want to summarize or click the cell in which you want to insert the sparkline.

2. On the **Insert** tab, in the **Sparklines** group, click **Line**, **Column**, or **Win/Loss** to specify the type of sparkline you want to create.

3. In the **Create Sparklines** dialog box, select, enter, or verify the data range and the location range. Then click **OK**.

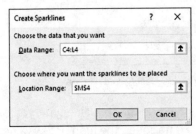

Create a sparkline in one cell and then copy it to others by using the fill feature

To enhance a selected sparkline

→ On the **Design** tool tab, do any of the following:

- In the **Show** group, select the check boxes for the data markers you want to show, and clear the check boxes for the data markers you want to hide.

- In the **Style** gallery, click the built-in style you want to apply.

- In the **Style** group, in the **Sparkline Color** gallery, click the color you want.

- In the **Style** group, in the **Marker Color** list, in the **Negative Points**, **Markers**, **High Point**, **Low Point**, **First Point**, and **Last Point** galleries, click the colors you want.

To change the type of a selected sparkline or sparkline group

→ On the **Design** tool tab, in the **Type** group, click the sparkline type you want.

To delete a sparkline or sparkline group

→ Select the sparkline you want to delete. On the **Design** tool tab, in the **Group** group, click the **Clear Selected Sparklines** button.

→ Select one or more sparklines in the sparkline group you want to delete. On the **Design** tool tab, in the **Group** group, click the **Clear Selected Sparklines** arrow, and then click **Clear Selected Sparkline Groups**.

2

Objective 2.4 practice tasks

The practice file for these tasks is in the **MOSExcel2019\Objective2** practice file folder. The folder also contains a result file that you can use to check your work.

➤ Open the **Excel_2-4** workbook. On the **Order Details** worksheet, use conditional formatting to do the following to all the values in the Extended Price column:

   ❑ Apply the *3 Arrows (Colored)* icon set. (Keep the default settings.)

   ❑ Add Blue data bars to the column. (Keep the default settings.)

   ❑ Fill all cells in the column that contain values greater than $100 with Yellow.

➤ On the **JanFeb** worksheet, do the following:

   ❑ Insert a row below the times. In that row, summarize the data for each hour by using a Column sparkline.

   ❑ Apply the *Colorful #4* sparkline style.

   ❑ Accentuate the First Point and Last Point data markers.

➤ On the **MarApr** worksheet, do the following:

   ❑ In column P, summarize the data for each day of March by using a Line sparkline.

   ❑ Apply the *Orange, Sparkline Style Accent 6, Darker 25%* style.

   ❑ Display all the data markers without placing emphasis on any specific type of data marker.

➤ Save the **Excel_2-4** workbook. Open the **Excel_2-4_results** workbook. Compare the two workbooks to check your work. Then close the open workbooks.

Objective group 3

Manage tables and table data

The skills tested in this section of the Microsoft Office Specialist exam for Microsoft Excel 2019 relate to creating tables. Specifically, the following objectives are associated with this set of skills:

3.1   Create and format tables

3.2   Modify tables

3.3   Filter and sort table data

An Excel table is a named object that has functionality beyond that of a simple data range. Some table functionality, such as the ability to sort and filter on columns, is also available for data ranges. Useful table functionality that is not available for data ranges includes the automatic application of formatting, the automatic copying of formulas, and the ability to perform the following actions:

- Quickly insert column totals or other mathematical results.

- Search for the named table object.

- Expose the named table object in a web view.

- Reference the table or any table field by name in a formula.

This chapter guides you in studying methods of creating and modifying tables, applying functional table formatting, and filtering and sorting data that is stored in a table.

Objective 3.1: Create and format tables

Create an Excel table from a cell range

The simplest way to create a table is by converting an existing data range. If you don't already have a data range, you can create a blank table and then add data to populate the table.

When you create a table from an existing data range, you choose the table format you want, and then Excel evaluates the data range to identify the cells that are included in the table and any functional table elements such as table header rows.

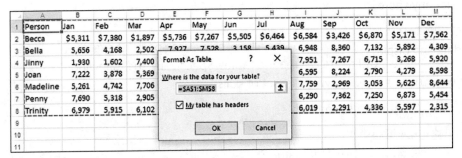

Excel evaluates the data range that contains the active cell

Each built-in table format you choose has specific functional elements built in to it, such as a header or banded (alternating) row formatting. You can choose the options you want to show on the table style thumbnails or modify the table options after you create the table.

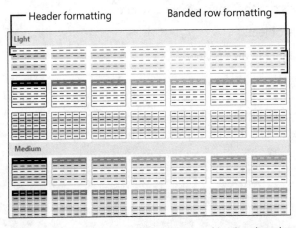

Choose from 60 preconfigured formatting combinations based on theme colors

Excel assigns a name to each table you create, based on its order of creation in the workbook (*Table1*, *Table2*, and so on). You can change the table name to one that makes it more easily identifiable (such as *Sales_2019*, *Students*, or *Products*).

IMPORTANT Names must begin with a letter or an underscore character. A name cannot begin with a number.

See Also For more information about naming and renaming tables, see "Objective 2.3: Define and reference named ranges."

To convert a data range to a table of the default style

1. Click anywhere in the data range.

2. On the **Insert** tab, in the **Tables** group, click **Table**. Excel selects the surrounding data and displays the Create Table dialog box.

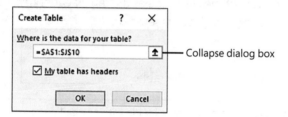

You can enter or select the table content

3. Verify that the cell range in the **Where is the data for your table** box is the cell range you want to convert to a table. If it isn't, do either of the following:

   • Correct the cell range in the dialog box by changing the letters and numbers.

   • Click the **Collapse Dialog Box** button to the right of the cell range, drag to select the cell range you want, and then click the **Expand Dialog Box** button to return to the full dialog box.

4. If you want to use the top row of the cell range as the table header row, verify that the **My table has headers** check box is selected.

5. In the **Create Table** dialog box, click **OK**.

To convert a data range to a table and select the table style

1. Click anywhere in the data range.

2. On the **Home** tab, in the **Styles** group, click **Format as Table**, and then click the table style you want.

3. In the **Format As Table** dialog box, do the following, and then click **OK**:

   a. Verify that the cell range in the **Where is the data for your table** box is the cell range you want to convert to a table. If it isn't, do either of the following:

      - Correct the cell range in the dialog box by changing the letters and numbers.

      - Click the **Collapse Dialog Box** button to the right of the cell range, drag to select the cell range you want, and then click the **Expand Dialog Box** button to return to the full dialog box.

   b. If you want to use the top row of the cell range as the table header row, verify that the **My table has headers** check box is selected.

To create an empty table

1. Select the cells in which you want to create the table.

Tip If you select only one cell, Excel creates a two-cell table with one cell designated for the header and one for the content.

---

2. On the **Home** tab, in the **Styles** group, click **Format as Table**, and then click the table style you want.

3. In the **Format As Table** dialog box, click **OK**.

To select a table

→ In the worksheet, do either of the following:

   - Point to the upper-left corner of the table. When the pointer changes to a diagonal arrow, click once to select the table.

   - Drag to select all cells of the table.

→ Click the **Name** box located at the left end of the formula bar to display a list of named objects, and then click the table.

Apply styles to tables

When you create a table, you apply a combination of formatting elements called a *table style*. The table style includes fonts, borders, and fills that are coordinated to provide a professional appearance. The available table styles are based on the worksheet theme colors. You can change the table style by choosing another from the Table Styles gallery.

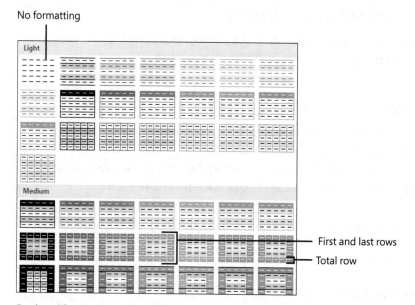

Excel modifies the style thumbnails based on the table options configured for the current table

To change the table style of the active table

1. On the **Design** tool tab, in the **Table Styles** group, do either of the following to expand the Table Styles menu:

   - If the gallery is visible, click the **More** button.

   - If the gallery is collapsed to a button, click the **Quick Styles** button.

2. In the **Table Styles** gallery, click the style you want.

To clear formatting from the active table

→ From the **Design** tool tab, expand the **Table Styles** menu, and then do either of the following:

- In the upper-left corner of the **Light** section of the gallery, click the **None** thumbnail.

- At the bottom of the menu, click **Clear**.

→ Select the table. On the **Home** tab, in the **Editing** group, click **Clear**, and then click **Clear Formats**.

Convert a table to a cell range

If you want to remove the table functionality from a table—for example, so you can work with functionality that is available only for data ranges and not for tables—you can easily convert a table to text. Simply converting the table doesn't remove any table formatting from the table; you can retain the formatting or clear it.

See Also For information about applying and clearing table formatting, see "Objective 3.2: Modify tables." For information about functionality that is specific to data ranges, see "Objective 2, Manage data cells and ranges."

To convert a table to a data range

1. Do either of the following:

   - Right-click anywhere in the table, click **Table**, and then click **Convert to Range**.

   - Select any cell in the table. Then on the **Design** tool tab, in the **Tools** group, click **Convert to Range**.

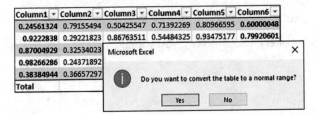

Converting a table removes functionality but not formatting

2. In the **Microsoft Excel** dialog box prompting you to confirm that you want to convert the table to a range, click **Yes**.

To remove table formatting from a data range

1. Select the data range.

2. On the **Home** tab, in the **Editing** group, click **Clear** and then **Clear Formats**.

3

Objective 3.1 practice tasks

The practice file for these tasks is in the **MOSExcel2019\Objective3** practice file folder. The folder also contains a result file that you can use to check your work.

➤ Open the **Excel_3-1** workbook. On the **2019 Sales** worksheet, do the following:

❑ Convert the data range B2:M23 to a table that includes a header row and uses *Table Style Medium 16*.

➤ On the **2020 Sales** worksheet, do the following:

❑ Change the table style to *Table Style Medium 19*.

➤ On the **Bonuses** worksheet, do the following:

❑ Convert the table to a data range.

❑ Remove the table formatting from the data range.

➤ Save the **Excel_3-1** workbook. Open the **Excel_3-1_results** workbook. Compare the two workbooks to check your work. Then close the open workbooks.

Objective 3.2: Modify tables

Add or remove table rows and columns

Inserting, deleting, or moving rows or columns in a table automatically updates the table formatting to gracefully include the new content. For example, adding a column to the right end of a table extends the formatting to that column, and inserting a row in the middle of a table that has banded rows updates the banding. You can modify the table element selections at any time.

To insert table rows and columns

→ To add a column to the right end of a table, click in the cell to the right of the last header cell, enter a header for the new column, and then press **Enter**.

→ To insert a single column within a table, do either of the following:

- Click a cell to the left of which you want to insert a column. On the **Home** tab, in the **Cells** group, click the **Insert** arrow, and then click **Insert Table Columns to the Left**.

- Select a table column to the left of which you want to insert a column (or select at least two contiguous cells in the column), and then in the **Cells** group, click the **Insert** button.

→ To insert multiple columns within a table, select the number of columns that you want to insert, and then in the **Cells** group, click the **Insert** button.

→ To insert a row at the bottom of the table, click in any cell in the row below the last table row, enter the text for that table cell, and then press **Tab**.

→ To insert a row within the table, do either of the following:

- Click a cell above which you want to insert a row. On the **Home** tab, in the **Cells** group, click the **Insert** arrow, and then click **Insert Table Rows Above**.

- Select a table row above which you want to insert a column (or select at least two contiguous cells in the row), and then in the **Cells** group, click the **Insert** button.

→ To insert multiple rows in a table, select the number of rows that you want to insert, and then in the **Cells** group, click the **Insert** button.

3

To move rows within a table

1. Select the table row(s) you want to move. (Do not select worksheet cells outside of the table.)

2. Point to the left edge of the selection until the cursor changes to a four-headed arrow.

3. Drag the selection to the new location (indicated by a thick green insertion bar).

Or

1. Select the worksheet row(s) that contain the table rows you want to move.

2. Point to the top or bottom edge of the selection until the cursor changes to a four-headed arrow.

3. Hold down the **Shift** key and drag the row to the new location (indicated by a thick gray insertion bar). Then release the **Shift** key.

Or

1. Select the worksheet row(s) that contain the table rows you want to move, and then cut the selection to the Clipboard.

2. Select the worksheet row above which you want to move the cut row or rows.

3. Do either of the following:

    - On the **Home** tab, in the **Cells** group, click the **Insert** arrow, and then click **Insert Cut Cells**.

    - Right-click the selected column, and then click **Insert Cut Cells**.

To move columns within a table

1. Select the table column(s) you want to move. (Do not select worksheet cells outside of the table.)

2. Point to the top of the selection until the cursor changes to a four-headed arrow.

3. Drag the selection to the new location (indicated by a thick green insertion bar).

Or

1. Select the worksheet column(s) that contain the table columns you want to move.

2. Point to the left or right edge of the selection until the cursor changes to a four-headed arrow.

3. Hold down the **Shift** key and drag the column(s) to the new location (indicated by a thick gray insertion bar). Then release the **Shift** key.

Or

1. Select the worksheet column(s) that contain the table columns you want to move, and then cut the selection to the Clipboard.

2. Select the worksheet column to the left of which you want to move the cut column or columns.

3. Do either of the following:

   - On the **Home** tab, in the **Cells** group, click the **Insert** arrow, and then click **Insert Cut Cells**.

   - Right-click the selected column, and then click **Insert Cut Cells**.

To delete table rows and columns

➜ Select one or more (contiguous) cells in each row or column you want to delete. On the **Home** tab, in the **Cells** group, click the **Delete** arrow, and then click **Delete Table Rows** or **Delete Table Columns**.

➜ Right-click a cell in the row or column you want to delete, click **Delete**, and then click **Table Columns** or **Table Rows**.

Configure table style options

The table style governs the appearance of standard cells, special elements, and functional table elements, including the following:

- **Header row** These cells across the top of the table are formatted to contrast with the table content, require an entry, and look like column titles, but are also used to reference fields in formulas.

- **Total row** These cells across the bottom of the table are formatted to contrast with the table content. They do not require an entry, but clicking in any cell displays a list of functions for processing the numeric contents of the table column. These include Average, Count, Count Numbers, Max, Min, Sum, StdDev, and Var, and a link to the Insert Function dialog box from which any function can be inserted in the cell.

Table element formatting is designed to make table entries or fields easier to differentiate, and include an emphasized first column, emphasized last column, banded rows, and banded columns.

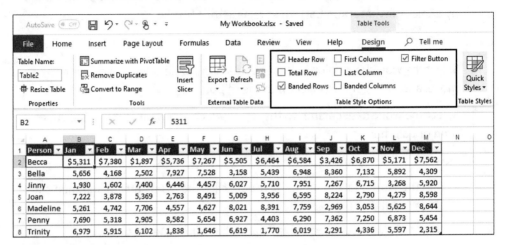

Configure formatting and functional options in the Table Style Options group

To enable row-specific table functionality

→ On the **Design** tool tab, in the **Table Style Options** group, do any of the following:

- To designate that the first row contains labels that identify the content below them, select the **Header Row** check box.

- To add a calculation row at the bottom of a table, select the **Total Row** check box.

- To hide or display filter buttons (arrow buttons) in the table header, clear or select the **Filter Button** check box.

Tip Excel automatically adds filter buttons when you format a data range as a table. The filter buttons are adjacent to the right margin of each table header cell. If table columns are sized to fit the column headers and you turn on filter buttons, the filter buttons might overlap the table header text until you resize the column.

To apply contrasting formatting to specific table elements

→ On the **Design** tool tab, in the **Table Style Options** group, do any of the following:

- To alternate row cell fill colors, select the **Banded Rows** check box.

- To alternate column cell fill colors, select the **Banded Columns** check box.

- To emphasize the content of the first table column (for example, if the column contains labels), select the **First Column** check box.

- To emphasize the content of the last table column (for example, if the column contains total values), select the **Last Column** check box.

Exam Strategy   Whenever you are instructed to apply consistent formatting to a table, do so using the table formatting commands, not the standard cell formatting commands, so the formatting will persist when the table expands.

To configure the function of a Total row

1. Click any cell of the Total row to display an arrow.

2. Click the arrow to display the functions that can be performed in the cell.

	A	B	C	D	E	F	G
1	Person	Jan	Feb	Mar	Apr	May	Jun
2	Becca	$ 5,311	$7,380	$1,897	$5,736	$7,267	$5,505
3	Bella	5,656	4,168	2,502	7,927	7,528	3,158
4	Jinny	1,930	1,602	7,400	6,446	4,457	6,027
5	Joan	7,222	3,878	5,369	2,763	8,491	5,009
6	Madeline	5,261	4,742	7,706	4,557	4,627	8,021
7	Penny	7,690	5,318	2,905	8,582	5,654	6,927
8	Trinity	6,979	5,915	6,102	1,838	1,646	6,619
9	Total						
10		None					
11		Average					
12		Count					
13		Count Numbers					
14		Max					
15		Min					
16		Sum					
		StdDev					
		Var					
		More Functions...					

Modify a Total row to perform other mathematical functions

3. In the list, click the function you want to perform in the cell.

4. To perform the same function in all cells of the row, copy the cell formatting to the rest of the row.

Objective 3.2 practice tasks

The practice file for these tasks is in the **MOSExcel2019\Objective3** practice file folder. The folder also contains a result file that you can use to check your work.

➤ Open the **Excel_3-2** workbook, and on the **Sales** worksheet, do the following:

❑ Configure the table style options to format alternating rows with different fill colors.

❑ Configure the table style options to emphasize the first column of the table.

❑ Move the *July* column so that it is between the *June* and *August* columns.

❑ Move the *Linda*, *Max*, and *Nancy* rows at one time so that they are between the *Kay* and *Olivia* rows.

❑ Insert a table row for a salesperson named **Raina** between the *Quentin* and *Steve* rows.

❑ Insert a column named **Dec** between the *Nov* and *Year* columns.

❑ Add a total row to the table.

❑ Change the total row name from *Total* to **Average**.

❑ Modify the cells in the *Average* row to calculate the average sales for each month and for the year.

❑ Delete the *Year* column from the table.

➤ Save the **Excel_3-2** workbook. Open the **Excel_3-2_results** workbook. Compare the two workbooks to check your work. Then close the open workbooks.

Objective 3.3: Filter and sort table data

You can easily sort and filter content in an Excel table. Sorting sets the order of the content, and filtering displays only rows containing entries that match the criteria you choose.

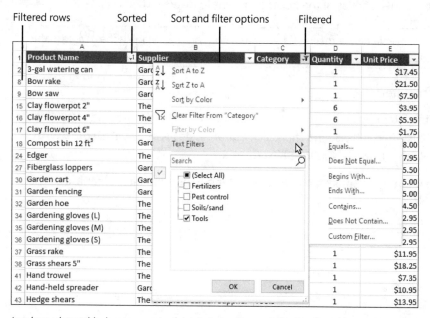

In a large data table, locate meaningful data by sorting and filtering the table content

Filter tables

You can filter a table by the content of one or more columns. You can filter to include or exclude rows that contain an exact match of a column entry, that contain specific text, or that have a specific font color. Filters can include wildcards such as ? (a question mark) to represent any single character or * (an asterisk) to represent a series of characters.

To filter a table to match a specific column entry

1. Click the filter button in the header of the column by which you want to filter the table.

2. At the top of the list of column entries, clear the **(Select All)** check box, and then select the check boxes of the items you want to display. Then click **OK**.

Tip You can enlarge the menu to display more options by dragging the handle in the lower-right corner of the menu.

To specify text filters

1. Click the filter button in the header of the column by which you want to filter the table, click **Text Filters**, and then click **Equals**, **Does Not Equal**, **Begins With**, **Ends With**, **Contains**, or **Does Not Contain**.

2. In the **Custom AutoFilter** dialog box, enter one or more filter criteria, and then click **OK**.

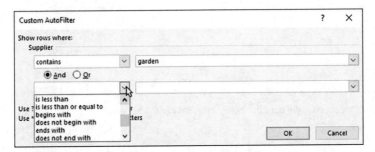

Custom filters can use two different criteria

To specify number filters

1. Click the filter button in the header of the column by which you want to filter the table, click **Number Filters**, and then click **Equals**, **Does Not Equal**, **Greater Than**, **Greater Than Or Equal To**, **Less Than**, **Less Than Or Equal To**, or **Between**.

2. In the **Custom AutoFilter** dialog box, enter one or more filter criteria, and then click **OK**.

To remove a filter

➔ In the table header, click the filter button, and then click **Clear Filter From *"Column"***.

To remove all filters from the active table

➔ On the **Home** tab, in the **Editing** group, click **Sort & Filter**, and then click the active **Filter** command or click **Clear**.

➔ Press **Ctrl+Shift+L**.

Sort tables

You can sort or filter on one column at a time by using the commands on the menu that appears when you click the filter button at the top of the column, or you can configure a multilevel sort from the Sort dialog box.

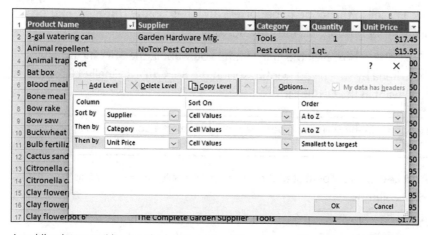

A multilevel sort provides a method of displaying different views of large amounts of data

By default, Excel assumes that the first row in the worksheet contains column headings and does not include it in the sort. It also assumes that you want to sort by the values in the table cells. You can sort values numerically or alphabetically in ascending or descending order. Standard sort orders are from A to Z for text, from smallest to largest for numbers, and from oldest to newest for dates. You can optionally sort by other features of the data range, including cell color, font color, and cell icon. These options are particularly useful in conjunction with conditional formatting.

You can also specify whether entries starting with uppercase and lowercase letters should be sorted separately and the orientation of the sort (whether you want to sort columns or rows).

Tip You can sort a table by the content of hidden columns within that table.

To sort a table by the values in one column

➜ At the right end of the column header, click the filter button, and then click the sort order you want.

To sort the active table by multiple columns

1. Do either of the following:

   • On the **Home** tab, in the **Editing** group, click the **Sort & Filter** button, and click **Custom Sort**.

   • Click any cell in the range to be sorted, and then on the **Data** tab, in the **Sort & Filter** group, click the **Sort** button.

2. In the **Sort** dialog box, click the first column you want in the **Sort by** list. Then click the criteria by which you want to sort in the **Sort on** list. Finally, click the order you want in the **Order** list.

   Tip The options in the Sort dialog box change if you select a Color or Icon option in the Sort On list.

3. Click **Add Level**, and repeat step 2 for the second column. Repeat this step for additional columns.

4. Click **OK**.

To change the sort order

➜ In the **Sort** dialog box, set the order for each of the sorting criteria.

➜ In the table header, click the active sort button to reverse the sort order.

Objective 3.3 practice tasks

The practice file for these tasks is in the **MOSExcel2019\Objective3** practice file folder. The folder also contains a result file that you can use to check your work.

➤ Open the **Excel_3-3** workbook, and on the **Bonuses** worksheet, do the following:

❑ Filter the table to display only the bonuses that were more than $2,500.00.

➤ On the **Products** worksheet, do the following:

❑ Sort the data by category (from A to Z) and, within each category, by unit price (from lowest to highest).

❑ Sort the data in descending order by category (from Z to A) and, within each category, by product name (from A to Z).

➤ Save the **Excel_3-3** workbook. Open the **Excel_3-3_results** workbook. Compare the two workbooks to check your work. Then close the open workbooks.

Perform operations by using formulas and functions

The skills tested in this section of the Microsoft Office Specialist exam for Microsoft Excel 2019 relate to the application of functions and formulas. Specifically, the following objectives are associated with this set of skills:

4.1 Insert references in formulas

4.2 Calculate and transform data by using functions

4.3 Format and modify text by using functions

Simple formulas and more complex functions provide the means to interpret raw data stored in a workbook in meaningful ways. They also provide a useful structure for processing information. You can increase the consistency and reliability of information by using formulas to calculate, evaluate, and express data.

You can calculate the data on a worksheet based on data in other areas of the workbook and in other workbooks. Excel maintains referential relationships when you move data or modify the data storage structure.

This chapter guides you in studying ways of referencing cells and ranges of cells both absolutely and relatively in formulas, and using formulas to sum and average cell values and count cells. It also guides you in processing data that meets specific conditions, and in manipulating text by using formulas.

4

Objective 4.1: Insert references in formulas

Insert relative, absolute, and mixed references

Formulas in an Excel worksheet usually involve functions performed on the values contained in one or more other cells on the worksheet (or on another worksheet). A reference that you make in a formula to the contents of a worksheet cell is either a *relative reference*, an *absolute reference*, or a *mixed reference*. It is important to understand the difference and know which to use when creating a formula.

A relative reference to a cell takes the form *A1*. When you copy or fill a formula from the original cell to other cells, a relative reference changes to maintain the relationship between the cell containing the formula and the referenced cell. For example, copying a formula that refers to cell A1 one row down changes the A1 reference to A2; copying the formula one column to the right changes the A1 reference to B1.

An absolute reference takes the form *$A$1*. The dollar sign indicates an absolute reference to the column or row designator that follows it. When you copy or fill a formula from the original cell to other cells, an absolute reference does not change—regardless of the relationship to the referenced cell, the reference stays the same.

	A	B	C	D	E	F
1			Customer	Wingtip Toys		
2			Discount	20%		
3						
4	Product	Toy plane				
5	Base price	$ 15.00				
6						
7	Order quantity	Quantity discount	Price (each)	Order subtotal	Customer discount	Order total
8	100	0%	$ 15.00	$ 1,500.00	$ 300.00	$ 1,200.00
9	200	5%	$ 14.25	$ 2,850.00	$ 570.00	$ 2,280.00
10	300					
11	400					
12	500					

	A	B	C	D	E	F
1			Customer	Wingtip Toys		
2			Discount	0.2		
3						
4	Product	Toy plane				
5	Base price	15				
6						
7	Order quantity	Quantity discount	Price (each)	Order subtotal	Customer discount	Order total
8	100	0	=$B$5-($B$5*B8)	=A8*C8	=D8*$D$2	=D8-E8
9	200	0.05	=$B$5-($B$5*B9)	=A9*C9	=D9*$D$2	=D9-E9
10	300	0.075	=$B$5-($B$5*B10)	=A10*C10	=D10*$D$2	=D10-E10
11	400	0.1	=$B$5-($B$5*B11)	=A11*C11	=D11*$D$2	=D11-E11
12	500	0.125	=$B$5-($B$5*B12)	=A12*C12	=D12*$D$2	=D12-E12

The customer discount is calculated by using an absolute reference to the discount percentage

See Also For information about showing formulas in a worksheet, see Objective 1.4, "Customize options and views."

A mixed reference refers absolutely to either the column or row and relatively to the other. For example, the mixed reference *A$1* always refers to row 1, and *$A1* always refers to column A.

Exam Strategy Exam MO-200 requires you to demonstrate only that you can reference cells on the same worksheet. Referencing cells on other worksheets and in other workbooks is part of the objective domain for Exam MO-201, Microsoft Excel Expert.

You can refer to the content of a range of adjacent cells. For example, you might use a formula to return the maximum value of all the cells in a row. When referencing a range of cells in a formula, the cell references can be relative, absolute, or mixed.

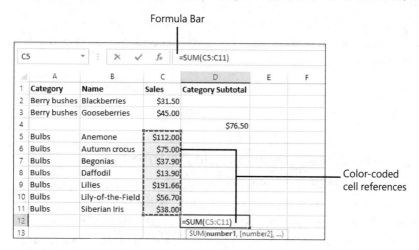

Selecting one or more cells creates a relative reference

To insert a cell or range reference into a formula

1. In the cell or formula bar, position the cursor within the formula where you want to insert the reference.

2. Use the reference procedure that corresponds to the type of reference you want to insert.

To relatively reference the contents of a cell

→ Enter the column letter followed by the row number, like this:

A1

To relatively reference the contents of a range of cells

➔ Enter the upper-left cell of the range and the lower-right cell of the range, separated by a colon, like this:

   A1:B3

➔ Drag to select the cell range and insert a relative reference to it.

To absolutely reference the contents of a cell

➔ Precede the column letter and row number by dollar signs, like this:

   $A$1

➔ Enter the relative reference, click in or select the reference, and then press **F4**.

To absolutely reference the contents of a range of cells

➔ Enter the upper-left cell of the range and the lower-right cell of the range, separated by a colon, and precede each column letter and row number by dollar signs, like this:

   $A$1:$B$3

➔ Enter the relative range reference, select the range, and then press **F4**.

Reference named cell ranges and tables in formulas

Coverage of Objective 2.3 includes information about naming and renaming cell ranges and tables. A primary reason for naming objects is so that you can easily reference them in formulas. When you compose a formula from the formula bar, named objects appear in a drop-down list as you enter the first characters of the name. You can select the object you want to reference from the list to avoid spelling errors.

Excel makes it easy to reference named objects and ranges

To reference a named range or table in a formula

1. In the formula, begin typing the range name or table name.

2. In the list that appears, select the named object you want to reference in the formula.

Objective 4.1 practice tasks

The practice file for these tasks is in the **MOSExcel2019\Objective4** practice file folder. The folder also contains result files that you can use to check your work.

➤ Open the **Excel_4-1** workbook, display the **Multiplication Table** worksheet, and do the following:

❑ Create a formula in cell B2 and copy the formula to the other cells in the range B2:K11 to complete the multiplication table of the numbers 1 through 10. Use mixed referencing to ensure that the formula works when copied.

➤ On the **Sales By Category** worksheet, do the following:

❑ In cell C7, calculate the Carnivorous sales total, using an absolute cell range reference. Then copy the formula to D7 so it returns the same result.

❑ In cells D17, D24, and D28, calculate the sales total for each category by using a relative cell range reference.

❑ In cell D29, use the simplest method to create a formula that returns the total sales for the four categories.

➤ Save the **Excel_4-1** workbook. Open the **Excel_4-1_results** workbook. Compare the two workbooks to check your work. Then close the open workbooks.

Objective 4.2: Calculate and transform data by using functions

Formulas in Excel can be made up of values that you enter, values that you reference (cell references, named ranges, named objects), mathematical operators, and the functions that ultimately structure and control the formula. A function can be thought of as a service provided by Excel to do a specific task. That task might be to perform a mathematical operation, to make a decision based on specific factors, or to perform an action on some text. A function is always indicated by the function name followed by a set of parentheses (for example, the SUM() function).

For most functions, arguments (variables) inside the parentheses either tell the function what to do or identify values for the function to work with. An argument can be a value that you enter, a cell reference, a range reference, a named range, a named object, or even another function. The number and type of arguments vary depending on which function you're using. Many functions allow optional arguments; these are indicated in function descriptions by square brackets. For example, =SUM(number1,[number2], [number3]) indicates that the SUM() function requires one number but accepts additional numbers. It is important to understand the syntax of common functions and to be able to correctly enter the function arguments. Fortunately, you don't have to memorize anything; the Formula AutoComplete feature leads you through the process of selecting the correct function name and entering the required arguments in the correct syntax.

Perform calculations by using the SUM(), AVERAGE(), MIN(), and MAX() functions

The following table describes the purpose of each of the functions that you can use to calculate data from a range of cells, and the types of arguments the functions accept.

Function	Purpose	Arguments
SUM()	Returns the total of the cell values	number1,number2,...,number255
AVERAGE()	Returns the average of the cell values	number1,number2,...,number255
MIN()	Returns the minimum value within the set	number1,number2,...,number255
MAX()	Returns the maximum value within the set	number1,number2,...,number255

Each of these functions takes up to 255 numeric arguments, which can be a number entered directly in the formula, a text representation of a number (a number inside of quotation marks), a cell reference, a range reference, or a named reference. The function ignores any cells that contain text that can't be translated to a number, that are empty, or that contain an error.

You can enter arguments directly in the formula structure, through a dialog box interface, by clicking to select cells, or by dragging to select ranges.

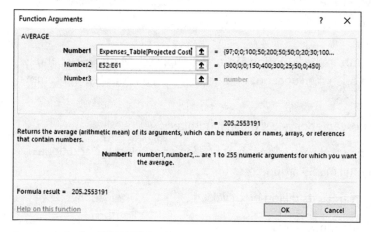

Arguments for the AVERAGE() function

Probably the most common formula used in Excel, and certainly the simplest to understand, is the SUM() function. The SUM() function returns the total value of a set of numbers. Rather than individually adding the values of all the cells you want to total, you can use the SUM function to perform this task.

Tip The results of the AVERAGE, COUNT, and SUM functions appear by default on the status bar when you select multiple cells (contiguous or separate) that contain numeric values. You can optionally display the Numerical Count, Minimum, and Maximum values.

To sum values

➜ In the cell or formula bar, enter the following formula, including up to 255 numbers, which can be in the form of cell references, a data range, or specific numbers:

=SUM(number1,[number2],[number3]...)

→ On the **Formulas** tab, in the **Function Library** group, click the **AutoSum** arrow (not the button), and then click **Sum**. Select or enter the numeric arguments you want to sum, and then press **Enter**.

→ In the **Function Library** group, click the **AutoSum** button (not the arrow) and press **Enter** to accept the logical range of values selected by Excel (the range immediately above or to the left of the active cell).

→ Click the **AutoSum** button. Click or drag to select the input values you want (press and hold **Ctrl** to select multiple cells and ranges). Then press **Enter**.

Or

1. On the **Formulas** tab, in the **Function Library** group, click **Math & Trig**, and then click **SUM** to open the Function Arguments dialog box displaying prompts for the SUM() function.

2. In the **Number1** box, enter or select the first number.

3. In the **Number2** box and each subsequent box, enter or select the additional numbers up to a total of 255 arguments.

4. In the **Function Arguments** dialog box, click **OK**.

To average values in a data range

→ In the cell or formula bar, enter the following formula, including up to 255 cell references or data ranges:

=AVERAGE(number1,[number2],[number3]...)

→ In the **Function Library** group, click the **AutoSum** arrow, and then click **Average**. Select or enter the cells you want to average, and then press **Enter**.

Or

1. In the **Function Library** group, click **More Functions**, click **Statistical**, and then click **AVERAGE** to open the Function Arguments dialog box displaying prompts for the AVERAGE() function.

2. In the **Number1** box, enter or select the first data range.

3. In the **Number2** box and each subsequent box, enter or select additional data ranges up to a total of 255 arguments.

4. In the **Function Arguments** dialog box, click **OK**.

To return the lowest value in a data range

→ In the cell or formula bar, enter the following formula, including up to 255 cell references or data ranges:

   =MIN(number1,[number2],[number3]...)

→ In the **Function Library** group, click the **AutoSum** arrow, and then click **Min**. Select or enter the cells you want to evaluate, and then press **Enter**.

Or

1. In the **Function Library** group, click **More Functions**, click **Statistical**, and then click **MIN** to open the Function Arguments dialog box displaying prompts for the MIN() function.

2. In the **Number1** box, enter or select the first data range.

3. In the **Number2** box and each subsequent box, enter or select additional data ranges up to a total of 255 arguments.

4. In the **Function Arguments** dialog box, click **OK**.

To return the highest value in a data range

→ In the cell or formula bar, enter the following formula, including up to 255 cell references or data ranges:

   =MAX(number1,[number2],[number3]...)

→ In the **Function Library** group, click the **AutoSum** arrow, and then click **Max**. Select or enter the cells you want to evaluate, and then press **Enter**.

Or

1. In the **Function Library** group, click **More Functions**, click **Statistical**, and then click **MAX** to open the Function Arguments dialog box displaying prompts for the MAX() function.

2. In the **Number1** box, enter or select the first data range.

3. In the **Number2** box and each subsequent box, enter or select additional data ranges up to a total of 255 arguments.

4. In the **Function Arguments** dialog box, click **OK**.

4

Count cells by using the COUNT(), COUNTA(), and COUNTBLANK() functions

The following table describes the purpose of each of the functions that you can use to count data from a range of cells, and the types of arguments the functions accept.

Function	Purpose	Arguments
COUNT()	Returns the number of cells that contain numeric values	*value1,value2,...,value255*
COUNTA()	Returns the number of cells that contain any content (are not empty)	*value1,value2,...,value255*
COUNTBLANK()	Returns the number of empty cells	*range*

Each of these functions takes up to 255 numeric arguments, either numbers or values, as follows:

- An argument specified as a number can be a number that is entered directly in the formula, a text representation of a number (a number inside of quotation marks), a cell reference, a range reference, or a named reference. The function ignores any cells that contain text that can't be translated to a number, that are empty, or that contain an error.

- An argument specified as a value can be any type of value. For example, the COUNT() function will evaluate the specified cells and return the count of only those that contain values it identifies as numbers, whereas the COUNTA() function will evaluate the cells and return the count of those that contain any content (are not blank).

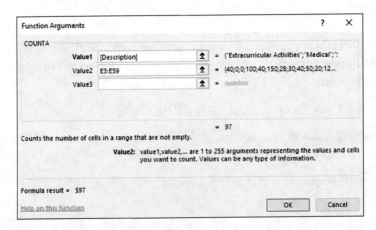

Arguments for the COUNTA() function

To count cells containing numeric values

→ In the cell or formula bar, enter the following formula, including up to 255 cell references or data ranges:

=COUNT(value1,[value2],[value3]...)

→ In the **Function Library** group, click the **AutoSum** arrow, and then click **Count Numbers**. Select or enter the cells you want to count, and then press **Enter**.

Or

1. In the **Function Library** group, click **More Functions**, click **Statistical**, and then click **COUNT**.

2. In the **Function Arguments** box, do the following, and then click **OK**.

   • In the **Value1** box, enter or select the first data range.

   • In the **Value2** box and each subsequent box, enter or select additional data ranges up to a total of 255 arguments.

To count non-empty cells

→ In the cell or formula bar, enter the following formula, including up to 255 cell references or data ranges:

=COUNTA(value1,[value2],[value3]...)

Or

1. In the **Function Library** group, click **More Functions**, click **Statistical**, and then click **COUNTA**.

2. In the **Function Arguments** box, do the following, and then click **OK**.

   • In the **Value1** box, enter or select the first data range.

   • In the **Value2** box and each subsequent box, enter or select additional data ranges up to a total of 255 arguments.

To count empty cells

→ In the cell or formula bar, enter the following formula, including up to 255 cell references or data ranges:

=COUNTBLANK(range)

4

Or

1. In the **Function Library** group, click **More Functions**, click **Statistical**, and then click **COUNTBLANK**.

2. In the **Function Arguments** box, enter or select the data range in the **Range** box, and then click **OK**.

Perform conditional operations by using the IF() function

You can use a formula to display specific results when certain conditions are met. To do so, you create a formula that uses conditional logic—specifically, the IF() function or one of its variations.

Exam Strategy   Exam MO-200 requires that you be able to demonstrate the use of the IF() function. Variants such as the SUMIF(), SUMIFS(), COUNTIF(),COUNTIFS(), AVERAGEIF(), and AVERAGEIFS() functions are part of the objective domain for Microsoft Office Specialist Exam MO-201, Microsoft Excel Expert.

A formula that uses conditional logic evaluates a specific condition and then returns one of two results based on whether the logical test evaluates as TRUE or FALSE.

The correct syntax for the IF() function is *IF(logical_test,value_if_true,value_if_false)*. For example, the following formula evaluates a student's grade in cell D4 and returns Pass if the grade is 70 or above and Fail if the grade is less than 70:

   =IF(D4<70,"Fail","Pass")

When using the IF() function, the logical test must be one that can have only a true or false result.

Tip   The IF() function in Excel is equivalent to an IF...THEN...ELSE function in a computer program.

The logical test and the results can include text strings or calculations. Enclose text strings within the formula in quotation marks.

Exam Strategy   You can nest multiple functions so that Excel evaluates multiple conditions before returning a result. You can add logical tests to a conditional formula by using the AND(), OR(), and NOT() functions. Nested functions and custom conditional formats are part of the objective domain for Microsoft Office Specialist Exam MO-201, Microsoft Excel Expert.

To return a value based on a conditional test

→ In the cell or formula bar, enter the following formula, where *logical_test* is the condition that must be met, *value_if_true* is the value the formula returns if the condition is met, and *value_if_false* is the value the formula returns if the condition is not met:

= IF(*logical_test,value_if_true,value_if_false*)

Or

1. On the **Formulas** tab, in the **Function Library** group, click **Logical**, and then click **IF** to open the Function Arguments dialog box displaying prompts for the IF() function.

2. In the **Logical_test** box, enter a pass/fail condition.

3. In the **Value_if_true** box, enter the value the formula will return if the condition is met. To return a text string, enclose it in quotes.

4. In the **Value_if_false** box, enter the value the formula will return if the condition is not met.

5. In the **Function Arguments** dialog box, click **OK**.

4

Objective 4.2 practice tasks

The practice file for these tasks is in the **MOSExcel2019\Objective4** practice file folder. The folder also contains a result file that you can use to check your work.

➤ Open the **Excel_4-2** workbook. On the **Sales By Region** worksheet, do the following:

❑ In cell A18, create a formula that returns the number of non-empty cells in the cell range named *Season*.

❑ In cell D5, create a formula that returns the average Sales value for the Fall season.

❑ In cell D9, create a formula that returns the maximum Sales value for the Spring season.

❑ In cell D13, create a formula that returns the minimum Sales value for the Summer season.

❑ In cell G2, create a formula that returns the average value in the cell range named *Sales*.

❑ In cell F5, use the IF function to display the text "Excellent sales season!" if D5 is higher than G2, and otherwise leaves the cell blank.

➤ Save the **Excel_4-2** workbook. Open the **Excel_4-2_results** workbook. Compare the two workbooks to check your work. Then close the open workbooks.

Objective 4.3: Format and modify text by using functions

Select text by using the LEFT(), MID(), and RIGHT() functions

You can use the formulas shown in the following table to return portions of cell content based on position.

Function	Description
LEFT()	Returns the leftmost character or characters of a text string
MID()	Returns a specific number of characters from a text string, starting at the position you specify
RIGHT()	Returns the rightmost character or characters of a text string

The LEFT(), MID(), and RIGHT() functions count each character in the specified text string. The LEFT() and RIGHT() functions take the following arguments:

- *text* (required) The text string to be evaluated by the formula.
- *num_chars* (optional) The number of characters to be returned. If *num_chars* is not specified, the function returns one character.

The syntax for the LEFT() and RIGHT() functions is:

LEFT(text,num_chars)

RIGHT(text,num_chars)

For example, the formula *=LEFT(Students[@[Last Name]],1)* returns the first letter of the student's last name.

The MID() function takes the following arguments:

- *text* (required) The text string to be evaluated by the formula.
- *start_num* (required) The position from the left of the first character you want to extract. If *start_num* is greater than the number of characters in the text string, the function returns an empty string.
- *num_chars* (required) The number of characters to be returned. If *num_chars* is not specified, the function returns one character.

4

The syntax for the MID() function is:

MID(text,start_num,num_chars)

	A	B	C
1	Phone	Area Code	Local Number
2	425-555-0100	425	=MID(A2,5,8)
3	206-555-0123	206	555-0123
4	972-555-0134	972	555-0134
5	858-555-0149	858	555-0149
6	360-555-0164	360	555-0164
7	619-555-0192	619	555-0192

The MID() function returns a specific number of characters from a text string

To return one or more characters from the left end of a text string

→ In the cell or formula bar, enter the following formula, where *text* is the source text and *num_chars* is the number of characters you want to return:

=LEFT(text,num_chars)

Or

1. On the **Formulas** tab, in the **Function Library** group, click **Text**, and then click **LEFT** to open the Function Arguments dialog box displaying prompts for the LEFT() function.

2. In the **Text** box, enter or select the source text.

3. In the **Num_chars** box, enter the number of characters you want to return.

4. In the **Function Arguments** dialog box, click **OK**.

To return one or more characters from within a text string

→ In the cell or formula bar, enter the following formula, where *text* is the source text, *start_num* is the character from which you want to begin returning characters, and *num_chars* is the number of characters you want to return:

=MID(text,start_num,num_chars)

Or

1. On the **Formulas** tab, in the **Function Library** group, click **Text**, and then click **MID** to open the Function Arguments dialog box displaying prompts for the MID() function.

2. In the **Text** box, enter or select the source text.

3. In the **Start_num** box, enter the character from which you want to begin returning characters.

4. In the **Num_chars** box, enter the number of characters you want to return.

5. In the **Function Arguments** dialog box, click **OK**.

To return one or more characters from the right end of a text string

→ In the cell or formula bar, enter the following formula, where *text* is the source text and *num_chars* is the number of characters you want to return:

   =RIGHT(text,num_chars)

Or

1. On the **Formulas** tab, in the **Function Library** group, click **Text**, and then click **RIGHT** to open the Function Arguments dialog box displaying prompts for the RIGHT() function.

2. In the **Text** box, enter or select the source text.

3. In the **Num_chars** box, enter the number of characters you want to return.

4. In the **Function Arguments** dialog box, click **OK**.

Format text by using the UPPER(), LOWER(), and PROPER() functions

You can use the formulas shown in the following table to return case-modified text. This is useful when you want to make data from a variety of sources consistent.

Function	Description
UPPER()	Converts text to uppercase
LOWER()	Converts text to lowercase
PROPER()	Capitalizes the first letter of each word in a text string

The UPPER(), LOWER(), and PROPER() functions each take only one argument: the text string to be processed. The syntax of the functions is:

UPPER(text)

LOWER(text)

PROPER(text)

To convert a text string to uppercase

➜ In the cell or formula bar, enter the following formula, where text is the source text:

> =UPPER(text)

Or

1. On the **Formulas** tab, in the **Function Library** group, click **Text**, and then click **UPPER**.

2. In the **Function Arguments** dialog box, enter or select the source text that you want to convert to uppercase, and then click **OK**.

To convert a text string to lowercase

➜ In the cell or formula bar, enter the following formula, where *text* is the source text:

> =LOWER(text)

Or

1. On the **Formulas** tab, in the **Function Library** group, click **Text**, and then click **LOWER**.

2. In the **Function Arguments** dialog box, enter or select the source text that you want to convert to lowercase, and then click **OK**.

To capitalize each word of a text string

➜ In the cell or formula bar, enter the following formula, where *text* is the source text:

> =PROPER(text)

Or

1. On the **Formulas** tab, in the **Function Library** group, click **Text**, and then click **PROPER**.

2. In the **Function Arguments** dialog box, enter or select the source text that you want to convert to lowercase, and then click **OK**.

Count characters by using the LEN() and LENB() functions

The LEN() function returns the number of characters within a specific cell (including spaces). This may be useful if you're developing text content in an Excel workbook; similar functionality is provided by the Word Count utility in Microsoft Word.

The LENB() function provides the same results for double-byte character set (DBCS) languages such Chinese, Japanese, and Korean.

The LEN() and LENB() functions each take only one argument: the text string to be processed. The syntax of the functions is:

LEN(text)

LENB(text)

Combine text by using the CONCAT() and TEXTJOIN() functions

You can use the formulas shown in the following table to join the contents of multiple cells.

Function	Description
CONCAT()	Concatenates up to 253 text components into one string
TEXTJOIN()	Concatenates up to 252 text components separated by a specified delimiter

IMPORTANT The CONCATENATE() function that was available in earlier versions of Excel has been replaced by the CONCAT() function. CONCATENATE() is available in Excel 2019 for backward compatibility but might not be available in future versions of Excel.

The CONCAT() and TEXTJOIN() functions can be very useful when working with text data. Using these functions, you can merge existing content from cells in addition to content that you enter in the formula.

The syntax for the CONCAT() function is:

CONCAT(text1,[text2],...)

The *[text]* arguments can be cell references, table column references, or text enclosed in double quotes.

For example, this formula returns a result such as *Smith, John: Grade 5*.

> =CONCAT(Table1[@[Last Name]],", ",Table1[@[First Name]],": Grade
> ", Table1[@Grade])

Tip You can use the ampersand (&) operator to perform the same process as the CONCAT() function. For example, =A1&B1 returns the same value as =CONCAT(A1,B1).

The TEXTJOIN() function is similar to CONCAT(), but also inserts a delimiter between the text strings you're concatenating, and has the option to exclude empty arguments from the concatenated results. The syntax for the TEXTJOIN() function is:

> *TEXTJOIN(delimiter,ignore_empty,text1,[text2],...)*

The delimiter is required; it can be a space or any character string enclosed in double quotes. You can have only one delimiter per formula.

The *ignore_empty* argument must be either TRUE or FALSE and specifies whether to return any empty results.

For example, this formula returns the name *Joan Elizabeth Lambert*:

> *TEXTJOIN(" ",TRUE,"Joan","Elizabeth","Lambert")*

To join multiple text strings in one cell

→ In the cell or formula bar, enter the following formula, including up to 253 text strings, which can be in the form of cell references or specific text enclosed in quotation marks:

> =CONCAT(text1,[text2],[text3]...)

Or

1. On the **Formulas** tab, in the **Function Library** group, click **Text**, and then click **CONCAT**.

2. In the **Function Arguments** dialog box, in the **Text1** box and each subsequent box, enter or select a cell reference or enter specific text. Then click **OK**.

To join and delimit multiple text strings in one cell

→ In the cell or formula bar, enter the following formula, including up to 255 text strings, which can be in the form of cell references or specific text enclosed in quotation marks:

=TEXTJOIN(delimiter,ignore_empty,text1,[text2],[text3]...)

Or

1. On the **Formulas** tab, in the **Function Library** group, click **Text**, and then click **TEXTJOIN** to open the Function Arguments dialog box displaying prompts for the TEXTJOIN() function.

2. In the **Delimiter** box, enter or select the character or characters you want the formula to insert between the text strings.

3. In the **Ignore_empty** box, enter TRUE if you want to omit empty arguments from the results or FALSE to return empty results between delimiters.

4. In the **Text1** box and each subsequent box, enter or select a cell reference or enter specific text.

5. In the **Function Arguments** dialog box, click **OK**.

4

Objective 4.3 practice tasks

The practice file for these tasks is in the **MOSExcel2019\Objective4** practice file folder. The folder also contains a result file that you can use to check your work.

➤ Open the **Excel_4-3** workbook. On the **Book List** worksheet, do the following:

❑ In the File By column, use a function to display the first two letters of the author's last name.

❑ In the AuthorID column, use a function to display the four characters in the middle of the AccountID (the letter followed by three numbers).

❑ In the Biography column, create a formula that displays a statement built from the BookTitle, AuthorFirst, AuthorLast, Publisher, and PubDate fields in the form *Microsoft Excel 2019 Step by Step by Curt Frye was published by Microsoft Press in 2018.* (including the period).

➤ Save the **Excel_4-3** workbook. Open the **Excel_4-3_results** workbook. Compare the two workbooks to check your work. Then close the open workbooks.

Objective group 5

Manage charts

The skills tested in this section of the Microsoft Office Specialist exam for Microsoft Excel 2019 relate to creating charts and objects. Specifically, the following objectives are associated with this set of skills:

- **5.1** Create charts
- **5.2** Modify charts
- **5.3** Format charts

You can store a large amount of data in an Excel workbook. When you want to present that data to other people, you might choose to present the data visually in the form of a chart. You can create many different types of charts in Excel 2019. To simplify the process of choosing a chart type, the Quick Analysis tool recommends charts that are most appropriate for the data you're working with.

Each chart you create is linked to the data that it represents. After you create a chart, you can modify it to include more or less data or to present the data differently. To help viewers interpret the chart data, you can configure a chart to include identifying elements such as a title, a legend, and data markers. You can apply these elements individually or as part of a predefined chart layout.

Charts you create within a workbook use the theme colors of that workbook. You can modify the colors in use, the assignment of colors to chart elements, and the graphic effects of the chart at one time by changing the chart style.

If you plan to distribute a workbook electronically, you should assign alt text (alternative descriptive text) to charts to assist viewers who have visual impairments or use screen-reading tools to interpret the meaning of the chart.

This chapter guides you in studying ways of presenting data in charts, moving charts to chart sheets, modifying chart content, displaying chart elements, applying chart layouts and chart styles, and providing alt text for charts.

5

Exam Strategy Exam MO-200 requires that you be able to demonstrate the ability to create charts based on data in ranges or tables. Creating PivotCharts from PivotTable data is part of the objective domain for Exam MO-201, Microsoft Excel Expert.

Objective 5.1: Create charts

Charts (also referred to as *graphs*) are created by plotting data points onto a two-dimensional or three-dimensional axis to assist in data analysis. Charts are commonly used to visually represent large data sets. Presenting data in the form of a chart can make it easy to identify trends and relationships that might not be obvious from the data itself.

Different types of charts are best suited for different types of data. The following table shows the available chart types and the data they are particularly useful for plotting.

Chart type	Typically used to show	Variations
Area	Multiple data series as cumulative layers showing change over time	Two-dimensional or three-dimensional Independent or stacked data series
Bar	Variations in value over time or the comparative values of several items at a single point in time	Two-dimensional or three-dimensional Stacked or clustered bars Absolute or proportional values
Box & Whisker	Distribution of data within a range, including mean values, quartiles, and outliers	
Column	Variations in value over time or comparisons	Two-dimensional or three-dimensional Stacked or clustered columns Absolute or proportional values
Funnel	Categorized numeric data such as sales or expenses	
Histogram	Frequency of occurrence of values within a data set	Optional Pareto chart includes additive contributions

Chart type	Typically used to show	Variations
Line	Multiple data trends over evenly spaced intervals	Two-dimensional or three-dimensional Independent or stacked lines Absolute or proportional values Can include markers
Map	A single series of geographic data	Two-color or three-color
Pie	Percentages assigned to different components of a single item (nonnegative, nonzero, no more than seven values)	Two-dimensional or three-dimensional Pie or doughnut shape Secondary pie or bar subset
Radar	Percentages assigned to different components of an item, radiating from a center point	Can include markers and fills
Stock	High, low, and closing prices of stock market activity	Can include opening price and volume traded
Sunburst	Comparisons of multilevel hierarchical data	
Surface	Trends in values across two different dimensions in a continuous curve, such as a topographic map	Two-dimensional or three-dimensional Contour or surface area
Treemap	Comparisons of multilevel hierarchical data	
Waterfall	The effect of positive and negative contributions on financial data	Optional connector lines
X Y (Scatter)	Relationships between sets of values	Data points as markers or bubbles Optional trendlines

5

You can also create combination charts (Combo charts) that overlay different data charts on one or multiple axes within the same plot area.

To plot data as a chart, you select the data and then select the chart type. Excel evaluates the pattern of the data and suggests chart types that typically represent similar data sets well, on the Charts tab of the Quick Analysis window and the Recommended Charts tab of the Insert Chart dialog box.

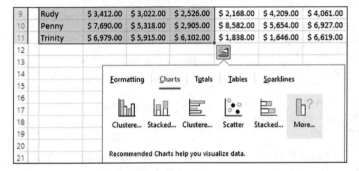

The Quick Analysis tool provides quick access to data transformation options

---

Tip The Quick Analysis tool provides access to formatting options that pertain to the currently selected data. From the tabs of the Quick Analysis tool, you can apply conditional formatting, perform mathematical operations, create tables and PivotTables, and insert sparklines. Like the Mini Toolbar, the Paste Options menu, and other context-specific tools, the Quick Analysis tool makes existing functionality available in a central location. The reason this is a tool rather than simply a toolbar or menu is that the options shown in the tool—for example, the charts shown on the Charts tab—are selected as appropriate for the current data.

In the Insert Charts dialog box, Excel also displays thumbnails representing the appearance of the selected data when rendered as each of the chart types, which makes it easy for you to review the options and select the one you want.

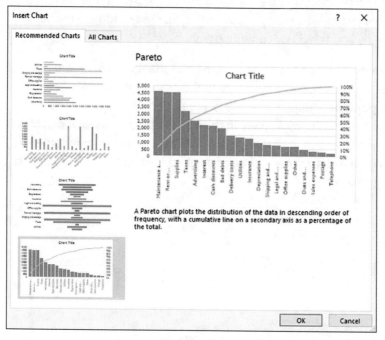

Excel displays the active data in each of the recommended chart thumbnails

You can select one of the recommended chart types, or select any type of chart from the Charts group on the Insert tab. On the Insert tab, a thumbnail is available for each variation of each chart type.

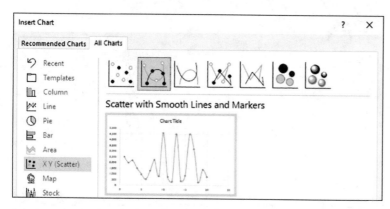

Select any chart type to display a thumbnail of each variation

5

Before you select the data that you want to present as a chart, ensure that the data is correctly set up for the type of chart you want to create (for example, you must set up hierarchical categories differently for a box & whisker, sunburst, or treemap chart than for a bar or column chart). Select only the data you want to appear in the chart. If the data is not in a contiguous range of rows or columns, either rearrange the data or hold down the Ctrl key while you select noncontiguous ranges.

By default, Excel creates charts on the same worksheet as the source data. You can move or size a chart on the worksheet by dragging the chart or its handles, or by specifying a precise position or dimensions. If you prefer to display a chart on its own sheet, you can move it to another worksheet in the workbook, or to a dedicated chart sheet. A chart sheet is similar to a worksheet in that it has a tab, but its only content is the chart. The chart on the chart sheet maintains a link to the chart data, so updating the data also updates the chart.

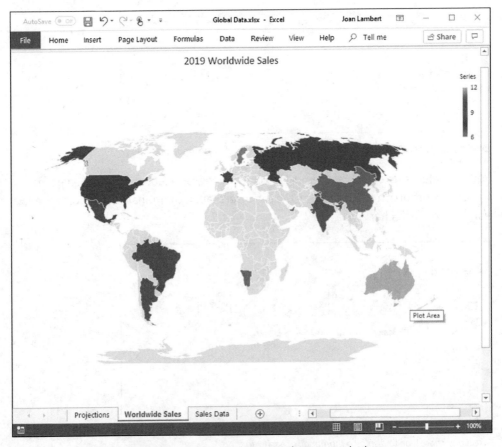

A chart sheet does not include standard worksheet elements such as rows and columns

To plot data as a chart on the worksheet

1. On the worksheet, select the data that you want to plot in the chart.

2. Do any of the following:

   - On the **Insert** tab, in the **Charts** group, click the general chart type you want, and then on the menu, click the specific chart you want to create.

     Tip Pointing to a chart type on the menu displays a live preview of the selected data plotted as that chart type.

   - On the **Insert** tab, in the **Charts** group, click **Recommended Charts**. Preview the recommended charts by clicking the thumbnails in the left pane. Click the chart type you want, and then click **OK**.

   - Click the **Quick Analysis** button that appears in the lower-right corner of the selection, click **Charts**, and then click the chart type you want to create.

To move a selected chart to a chart sheet

1. On the **Design** tool tab, in the **Location** group, click **Move Chart**.

2. In the **Move Chart** dialog box, select **New sheet**.

3. In the **New sheet** box, enter a name for the chart sheet.

Move a chart to its own sheet to remove the distraction of the background data

4. Click **OK** to simultaneously create the chart sheet and move the chart.

Objective 5.1 practice tasks

The practice file for these tasks is in the **MOSExcel2019\Objective5** practice file folder. The folder also contains a result file that you can use to check your work.

➤ Open the **Excel_5-1** workbook. On the **Seattle** worksheet, do the following:

❑ Plot the air quality data as a simple two-dimensional pie chart. Do not include the Total row in the charted data.

➤ On the **October Sales** worksheet, do the following:

❑ Plot the sales data as a clustered bar chart. Do not include the Total row or percentages.

➤ From the **Fall Sales** worksheet, do the following:

❑ Move the chart to a new chart sheet named *Fall Sales Chart*.

➤ Save the **Excel_5-1** workbook. Open the **Excel_5-1_results** workbook. Compare the two workbooks to check your work. Then close the open workbooks.

Objective 5.2: Modify charts

Modify chart content

A chart is linked to its worksheet data, so any changes you make to the plotted data are immediately reflected in the chart. If you want to add or delete values in a data series or add or remove an entire series, you need to increase or decrease the range of the plotted data in the worksheet.

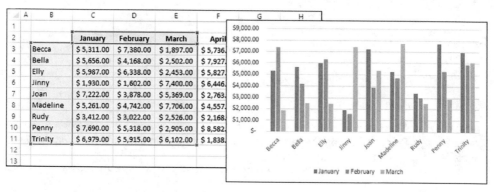

Change a chart by including more or less data

Sometimes a chart does not produce the results you expect because the data series are plotted against the wrong axes; that is, Excel is plotting the data by row when it should be plotting by column, or vice versa. You can quickly switch the rows and columns to see whether that produces the desired effect. You can preview the effect of switching axes in the Change Chart Type dialog box.

You can present a different view of the data in a chart by switching the data series and categories across the axis.

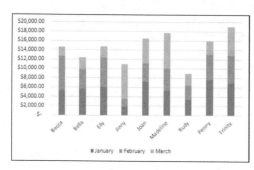
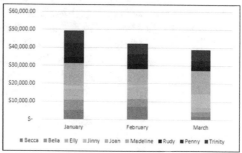

Change a chart by switching the data series and categories

You can swap data across the axis from the Change Chart Type dialog box, or you can more precisely control the chart content from the Select Data Source dialog box.

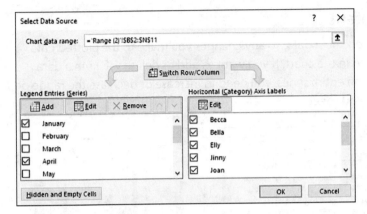

Choosing the data to include in a chart

Exam Strategy Practice plotting the same data in different ways. In particular, understand the effects of plotting data by column or by row.

To modify the data points in a chart

→ In the linked Excel worksheet, change the values within the chart data.

To select the chart data on the linked worksheet

→ Click the chart area or plot area.

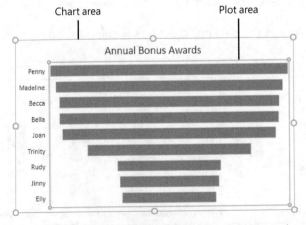

Selecting data on the chart selects the corresponding data on the worksheet

To change the range of plotted data in a selected chart

→ In the linked Excel worksheet, drag the corner handles of the series selectors until they enclose the series you want to plot.

Or

1. Do either of the following:

   - On the **Design** tool tab, in the **Data** group, click **Select Data**.
   - Right-click the chart area or plot area, and then click **Select Data**.

2. In the **Select Data Source** dialog box, do either of the following:

   - Click the worksheet icon at the right end of the **Chart data range** box, and then drag to select the full range of data you want to have available.
   - In the **Legend Entries (Series)** list and **Horizontal (Category) Axis Labels** boxes, select the check boxes of the rows and columns of data you want to plot.

3. In the **Select Data Source** dialog box, click **OK**.

To plot additional data series in a selected chart

1. Do either of the following:

   - On the **Design** tool tab, in the **Data** group, click **Select Data**.
   - Right-click the chart area or plot area, and then click **Select Data**.

2. In the **Select Data Source** dialog box, at the top of the **Legend Entries (Series)** list, click **Add**.

3. In the **Edit Series** dialog box, do either of the following:

   - Enter the additional series in the **Series name** box.
   - Click in the **Series name** box and then drag in the worksheet to select the additional series.

4. If necessary, enter or select the series values. Then click **OK**.

5. In the **Select Data Source** dialog box, click **OK**.

To switch the display of a data series in a selected chart between the series axis and the category axis

→ On the **Design** tool tab, in the **Data** group, click the **Switch Row/Column** button.

5

Or

1. Do either of the following:

    - On the **Design** tool tab, in the **Data** group, click **Select Data**.

    - Right-click the chart area or plot area, and then click **Select Data**.

2. In the **Select Data Source** dialog box, click **Switch Row/Column**, and then click **OK**.

Modify chart elements

A chart includes many elements, some required and some optional. The chart content can be identified by a *chart title*. Each data series is represented in the chart by a unique color. A *legend* that defines the colors is created by default but is optional. Each data point is represented in the chart by a data marker, and can also be represented by a *data label* that specifies the data point value. The data is plotted against an x-axis (or *category axis*) and a y-axis (or *value axis*). Three-dimensional charts also have a z-axis (or *series axis*). The axes can have titles, and gridlines can more precisely indicate the axis measurements.

To augment the usefulness or the attractiveness of a chart, you can add elements. You can adjust each element in appropriate ways, in addition to adjusting the plot area (the area defined by the axes) and the chart area (the entire chart object). You can move and format most chart elements, and easily add or remove them from the chart.

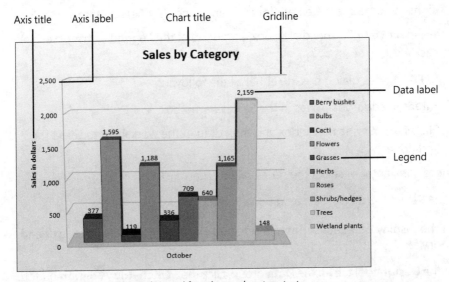

Chart elements can eliminate the need for other explanatory text

> **Tip** Data labels can clutter up all but the simplest charts. If you need to show the data for a chart on a separate chart sheet, consider using a data table instead.

You can add and remove chart elements from the Chart Elements pane or from the Design tool tab.

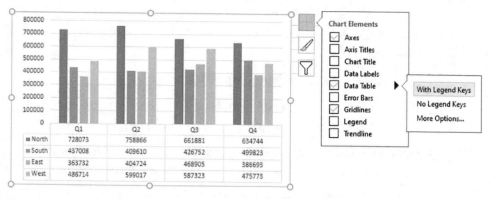

The options in the Chart Elements pane vary based on the chart type

Exam Strategy You can tailor the elements of charts in too many ways for us to cover them in detail here. In addition to choosing options from galleries, you can open a Format dialog box for each type of element. Make sure you are familiar with the chart elements and how to use them to enhance a chart.

To display and hide chart elements

➜ Click the chart, and then click the **Chart Elements** button (labeled with a plus sign) that appears in the upper-right corner of the chart. In the **Chart Elements** pane, select the check boxes of the elements you want to display, and clear the check boxes of the elements you want to hide.

➜ On the **Design** tool tab, in the **Chart Layouts** group, click **Add Chart Element**, click the element type, and then click the specific element you want to display or hide.

➜ On the **Design** tool tab, in the **Chart Layouts** group, click **Quick Layout**, and then click the combination of elements you want to display.

5

Objective 5.2 practice tasks

The practice file for these tasks is in the **MOSExcel2019\Objective5** practice file folder. The folder also contains a result file that you can use to check your work.

➤ Open the **Excel_5-2** workbook. On the **Fall Sales** worksheet, do the following:

❑ Switch the rows and columns of the chart.

❑ Change the October sales amount for the Flowers category to **500.00** and ensure that the chart reflects the change.

❑ Expand the data range plotted by the chart to include October and November, so that you can compare sales for the three months.

❑ Add the chart title *Sales by Category* above the chart.

❑ Above the chart, below the chart title, insert a legend that identifies the color that represents each month.

➤ Save the **Excel_5-2** workbook. Open the **Excel_5-2_results** workbook. Compare the two workbooks to check your work. Then close the open workbooks.

Objective 5.3: Format charts

Apply layouts and styles

You can apply predefined combinations of chart layouts and chart styles to quickly format a chart.

Chart layouts are predefined combinations and arrangements of chart elements. If all the elements you want to present for a chart are part of a chart layout, you can save time and ensure consistency by applying the chart layout instead of displaying and hiding individual chart elements.

Chart styles are predefined formatting options. Like other Microsoft Office styles, they use the workbook theme colors so you can feel confident when using a chart style that it will always coordinate with other theme-driven elements in the workbook. Each chart style assigns a selection of colors and graphic styles to the chart elements. Chart styles can modify the chart background and elements in ways that present either two-dimensional or three-dimensional views of the data.

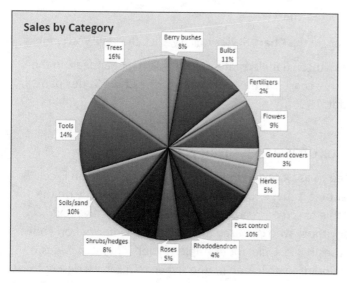

Preset formatting options make it easy to achieve the look you want

If the chart you initially create doesn't depict your data the way you want, you can change the chart type or select a different variation of the chart. Many chart types have two-dimensional and three-dimensional variations or optional elements.

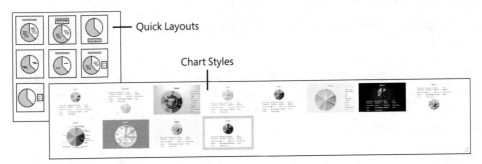

You can quickly make changes to the content and appearance of a chart

To change the layout of a selected chart

→ On the **Design** tool tab, in the **Chart Layouts** group, click **Quick Layout**, and then click the layout you want.

To change the style of a selected chart

→ On the **Design** tool tab, in the **Chart Styles** gallery, click the style you want.

→ Click the **Chart Styles** button (labeled with a paintbrush) that appears in the upper-right corner of the chart. On the **Style** page of the **Chart Styles** pane, click the style you want.

Provide alternative text for accessibility

Alternative text (also referred to as *alt text*) is descriptive text assigned to an Excel table, chart, image, or other object that either might not show up correctly on the page or might not be available to screen-reading software. The alternative text provides readers, particularly those who can't see the object, with information about the object content or purpose. In a PDF file, for example, if your content includes alternative text, a reader can point to an image on the screen to display a description of the image.

Some images, such as logos, are not necessary for an unsighted reader to review. In these instances, you can mark them as decorative and a screen reader will ignore them or announce them as decorative. This is more common in Microsoft Office apps such as PowerPoint than in Excel, but the feature is the same throughout all the Office apps.

To add alternative text to a chart

1. Select the chart. On the **Format** tool tab, in the **Accessibility** group, click **Alt Text**.

2. In the **Alt Text** pane, enter a description of the chart that provides the information that would be necessary for a person who could not see the chart to understand it. Excel automatically saves the alt text.

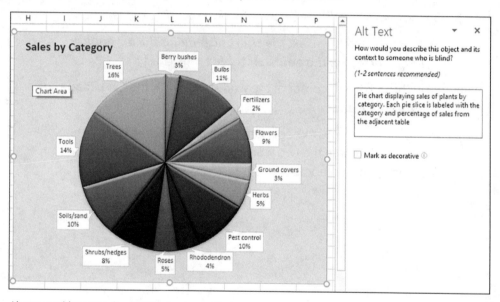

Alt text provides a text description of a visual object

To instruct a screen reader to ignore an image

1. Select the chart. On the **Format** tool tab, in the **Accessibility** group, click **Alt Text**.

2. In the **Alt Text** pane, select the **Mark as decorative** check box.

Objective 5.3 practice tasks

The practice file for these tasks is in the **MOSExcel2019\Objective5** practice file folder. The folder also contains a result file that you can use to check your work.

➤ Open the **Excel_5-3** workbook, display the **Sales** worksheet, and do the following:

❑ Apply the *Layout 1* Quick Style to the chart.

❑ Apply *Style 12* (the last preset style) to the chart.

➤ On the **Seattle** worksheet, do the following:

❑ Add the alternative text ***Pie chart displaying the air quality indicators from the adjacent table*** to the chart.

❑ In the upper-left corner of the worksheet, mark the lung image as decorative.

➤ Save the **Excel_5-3** workbook. Open the **Excel_5-3_results** workbook. Compare the two workbooks to check your work. Then close the open workbooks.

Index

Plug into learning at

MicrosoftPressStore.com

The Microsoft Press Store by Pearson offers:

- Free U.S. shipping

- Buy an eBook, get three formats – Includes PDF, EPUB, and MOBI to use with your computer, tablet, and mobile devices

- Print & eBook Best Value Packs

- eBook Deal of the Week – Save up to 50% on featured title

- Newsletter – Be the first to hear about new releases, announcements, special offers, and more

- Register your book – Find companion files, errata, and product updates, plus receive a special coupon* to save on your next purchase